TEACHING READING
THROUGH
MOTOR LEARNING

TEACHING READING
THROUGH
MOTOR LEARNING

By

DOROTHY D. SULLIVAN

*Associate Professor of Education and
Reading Specialist*

and

JAMES H. HUMPHREY

*Professor of Physical Education and
Motor Activity Learning Specialist*

*University of Maryland
College Park, Maryland*

With a Foreword by

R. M. W. Wilson

*Director of the Reading Center
College of Education
University of Maryland*

CHARLES C THOMAS • PUBLISHER
Springfield • Illinois • U.S.A.

Published and Distributed Throughout the World by

CHARLES C THOMAS • PUBLISHER
BANNERSTONE HOUSE
301–327 East Lawrence Avenue, Springfield, Illinois, U.S.A.

© 1973, by CHARLES C THOMAS • PUBLISHER

ISBN: 0–398–02732–3

Library of Congress Catalog Card Number: 72–92180

Printed in the United States of America

BB-14

FOREWORD

TEACHING READING THROUGH MOTOR LEARNING is a significant text for all of us to examine. Based on a strong background of research and theory, the authors have developed the strongest possible case for the inclusion of motor learning activities in the reading curriculum.

As one reads this text he will be acutely aware that these authors not only write a good line, but that they have provided application of their ideas to numerous situations. Teachers will find classroom examples which are field tested. Researchers will find logical "next steps" based upon the findings of others in the area of motor learning. Curriculum makers will find ample support for changes as well as specific suggestions. Teachers who work with problem readers will delight in the many suggestions contained in this text and in the authors' previous text, *TEACHING SLOW LEARNERS THROUGH ACTIVE GAMES.*

The text previously cited and this one should be viewed as a companion set. Reading one without the other will surely leave one with just a portion of the total value. This writer suggests reading *TEACHING READING THROUGH MOTOR LEARNING* first. It sets the stage, builds the case, and encourages one to read further.

After setting the case in the first three chapters, the authors make specific application of motor learning theory to the various aspects of reading, perceptual-motor development in Chapter Four, reading skills in Chapter Five, reading content in Chapter Six, creativity in Chapter Seven, and diagnosis in Chapter Eight.

Having witnessed the development of this text, this writer must add several comments on the diligence of the authors. One, a scholar in the area of motor activity and the other, a

v

skilled practitioner in the field of reading have combined forces to provide for the most impact. The care and concern they took to represent their respective fields accurately and to interpret the meeting of these two fields is highly commendable. Such teaming is a rarity in education; however, in this day when multidisciplinary references abound, these authors have set a fine model.

TEACHING READING THROUGH MOTOR LEARNING is the type of text you will read, reread, and refer to often. I'm certain it will find a proud place on your book shelf.

ROBERT M. WILSON

PREFACE

THROUGH READING THE individual receives the thoughts and feelings of others. Thus, reading, although multidimensional and "active" in nature, is considered as "passive," a receptive phase of language. In this case the word *receptive* might well carry a figurative as well as a purely literal meaning. Indeed, reading has been on the "receiving" end of a great deal of criticism during the past few years. Perhaps more criticism has been directed at reading than all of the other school curriculum areas combined. Although it may be difficult to determine precisely why reading has suffered the brunt of attack, one could speculate that it might be due to the fact that, in general, most people tend to consider reading as the real test of learning.

A good bit of the controversy involving reading seems to have focused around two general areas. First, there has been criticism of the various methods of teaching reading and second, there has been some question regarding the validity of the principles upon which these methods are based. Research studies are indicating that any method used in absolute form to the exclusion of all other methods would not meet the needs of all children. It is becoming increasingly evident that the procedures, or combination of procedures, employed should be those which best meet the needs of an individual child or a particular group of children. Such instruction then needs to be a response to the learning-to-read process as well as to the way children learn.

It is a well-known fact that an inordinately large number of books on reading have been published in recent years. People who use these books will generally testify to the fact that the books are much more alike than they are different and that there is really "little that is new" in such publications.

TEACHING READING THROUGH MOTOR LEARNING is characterized by its uniqueness. That is, the materials presented in this volume are intended to capitalize on the *physical* aspect of personality. This is to say that emphasis is placed on *motor learning* where motor components of the human organism are operating at a higher level than may be the case in more traditional *ideational* or *verbal* learning. Thus, the major thrust of the book is in the direction of learning to read through motor activity.

Chapter One introduces the concept generally, while Chapter Two provides a theoretical basis for the approach, along with some exploratory evidence to support it. Chapter Three takes into account some aspects of a motor nature that are inherent in and essential to the reading process.

When dealing with the physical aspect of personality as it relates to learning, one needs to take into account what has been termed education *of* the physical and education *through* the physical. Chapter Four which is concerned with perceptual-motor development and reading, might well be thought of as education *of* the physical, while Chapters Five, Six, Seven, and Eight are concerned with education *through* the physical. These final four chapters outline detailed information along with examples on how to help children with the various important factors concerned with reading. The focus is on developing reading skills through motor activity, motor-oriented reading content, learning to read through creative movement, and motor activity as it involves diagnosis and diagnostic teaching in reading.

This book should have a variety of uses. It could be helpful as a supplementary text in graduate courses in reading as well as in teacher preparation courses involving Teaching of Reading and in the area of Special Education. It should be valuable for reading specialists who serve as resource teachers for reading programs. Finally, it should be useful as a handbook of desirable learning activities and experiences for teachers.

The materials have undergone extensive field trials in various types of school situations. The authors are most grateful to the many teachers who worked with the various motor-oriented approaches presented in the book and made valuable suggestions for their use.

D.D.S.

College Park, Maryland

J.H.H.

CONTENTS

TEACHING READING
THROUGH
MOTOR LEARNING

INTRODUCTION

THE EVOLVING NATURE OF READING INSTRUCTION

WRITERS OF BASIC texts in reading frequently review the evolving nature of reading instruction and then proceed to present practices that are currently in evidence in our schools. The research relating to specific approaches or methods, materials, and types of children are also summarized. The usual caution is given in terms of the validity of these various research studies because of the myriad problems inherent in behavioral science research. It is a real concern of all the segments of our society who in some way are responsible for the educative processes of our institutions of learning that instructional approaches and materials, both old and new, be evaluated as to *how* and *when* and with *whom* they will be most effective in helping us move toward our educational objectives relating to reading. Many changes are anticipated in evaluation procedures in the coming years as we strive for more effective instruction and accountability. But regardless of the problems of the task, efforts to measure the effectiveness of instructional practices will and must continue.

Whenever innovations in instruction are recommended there is always concern that these innovations are consistent with what is now known about child growth and development as well as principles of learning. This is rightly so. As these innovations are being tried, there must also be an evaluation of their effectiveness in terms of educational objectives. The subsequent chapters of the book will therefore focus upon the theoretical basis of the *physical* aspect of the total personality and learning to read, along with

3

specific use of motor learning in such areas of reading as teaching children to read, diagnosing reading readiness and reading ability, and assisting the disabled reader In addition, some research will be alluded to in support of the theoretical perspectives.

Despite recurring admonitions as to the dangers of trying the "new" simply to be able to be identified as having innovative and progressive programs, there pervades throughout the literature a sense of urgency for new approaches and materials, different and more effective uses of the old approaches and materials, adaptive combinations of the old and new—something different, something that will work better than what our current reading instruction programs are producing. Wilson and Hall remind us of this need:

> "Much is known about reading, but our knowledge is not yet so complete that we can give each new teacher a model that he can use with assurance as an accepted organized body of data with which to correlate all his teaching and observations of reading. Each teacher must realize that his overview of the field can be only a tentative one."[1]

These authors go on to emphasize that meaningful programs of reading instruction for children must be based on the teacher's understanding of the reading process and "an open-minded receptivity to new developments."[2]

In the Sixty-seventh Yearbook, Part II, Congreve discusses implementing and evaluating the use of innovations. Starting from the basic premise that change can be desirable, he proceeds to develop a five-point rationale for sensible change. His dimensions for innovation and change in school include:

> "First, the faculty commits itself to the best educational program possible for the children and youth in the school. Second, they take a lifelong vow against blindly following every new idea. Third, they commit themselves to a continuing study of the school program in order to be aware of the strengths and weaknesses at all times. Fourth, as they consider courses of action, they become aware of the many alternatives available, they become knowledgeable about the effectiveness of such innovations as they have practiced in other situations, and they incorporate study and evaluation as part of in-

[1] Wilson, Robert M., and Hall, MaryAnne: *Reading and the Elementary School Child.* New York, Van Nostrand Reinhold Company, 1972, p. 4.
[2] *Ibid.*

troducing the innovation. Finally, the faculty does not give its exclusive attention to those aspects of the curriculum which seem to be getting attention from outside sources."[3]

It is all too clear that representatives of all segments of the nation's society are concerned about the effectiveness of the reading instruction programs of our schools. The national "Right to Read" program is particularly important because of its broad base of support of professionals and laymen. This program reflects the concerns of many, the relevancy and efficacy of present reading instruction practices in terms of meeting the needs of our young citizens from their many and varied backgrounds. Such programs are looking for answers from both the old and the innovative. But the message of the program is that we must try and we must find answers.

IMPORTANCE OF LEARNING THROUGH MOTOR ACTIVITY

There is also evidence from the literature of the direction that educators, psychologists, neurologists, sociologists and others are proposing for our improved programs of reading instruction, which also reflect their specific areas of expertise. It is interesting to note that their descriptions of what constitutes the appropriate learning environment for the child consistently reflect the *physical* aspect of total personality development presented in *Chapter Two*. The *physically*-oriented world of children is alluded to in descriptions of learning activities in general and in developing reading skills with comprehension in particular.

In *The Relevance of Education,* Bruner elaborates upon his concept of the spiraling curriculum by stating:

"It has been true of various curriculum projects that their success depended upon the invention of appropriate embodiments of ideas in these three modes—in action, image, and symbol. The balance beam, the pendulum, the proper set of modular blocks, the well-designed game or role play, the right vivarium or culture of growing yeast cells, the study of the proper tribal group—these may be

[3] Congreve, Willard J.: Implementing and evaluating the use of innovations. Robinson, Helen M. (Ed.): Innovations and Change in Reading Instruction, the *Sixty-seventh Yearbook of the National Society for the Study of Education*, Part II, Chicago, The University of Chicago Press, 1968, pp. 298–99.

high technological achievements in education. In time, one visits and revisits the same general principles, rendering them increasingly more abstract and formal, more precise, more powerful, more generative."[4]

In *Perceiving, Behaving, Becoming: A New Focus for Education,* the Association for Supervision and Curriculum Development in its 1962 Yearbook offers a challenge for new insights on the psychological aspect of educational programs with related implications for the social and philosophical aspects of the education process:

> "Schools are challenged to provide a balance of opportunities for non-verbal experiences, for a greater variety of visual, tactile and auditory devices. Firsthand experiences should implement abstract study. Children need time to explore the meaning of sound and motion, taste and touch. There should be many opportunities to enjoy feelings, to savor new sensory experiences. School programs which emphasize exclusively abstract learning and skill development, limit the development of sensing and feeling which are also a part of the process of becoming."[5]

In speaking specifically of the natural thrust of motivation in beginning first grade children, there is also awareness of the *physical* world of the learner.

> "There is an almost limitless desire to 'know,' to find out about things. Those who have worked with first graders are familiar with their requests: 'Let me see it;' 'Let me try;' 'Let me taste;' and so on and on. Here the whole world of things and people is their subject matter and they research it in their own way. They are aware of their limited experience and are eager to use all of their natural resources to 'see' what the unknown is like."[6]

Murray presents evidence of several new kinds of intrinsic motives—sensory, curiosity, activity, manipulatory, and cognitive which also relate to *physical* aspects of the learner. He cites

---

[4] Bruner, Jerome S.: *The Relevance of Education.* New York, W.W. Norton and Company, Inc., 1971, p. 122.

[5] Association for Supervision and Curriculum Development: *Perceiving, Behaving, Becoming: A New Focus for Education, Yearbook 1962.* Combs, Arthur W. (Chairman), ASCD 1962 Yearbook Committee, NEA, Washington, D.C., p. 238.

[6] *Ibid.,* p. 87.

the *sensory deprivation* studies begun at McGill University which refute those theories of motivation that hold the organism basically seeks to reduce stimulation. While people seek to avoid excessive environmental stimulation and inner tension, the students in the study found the state of nirvana intolerable.

> "They wanted stimulation so badly that they would ask to hear a recording of an old stock market report over and over again. Although they were asked to stay as long as possible, most subjects could take it for only two or three days. They preferred to work harder at less pay, in a stimulating environment."[7]

Behavior of the subjects during the sensory deprivation period was that of being unable to concentrate or sustain a train of thought after their initial attempts to think about personal and intellectual problems. They also had periods of confusion, irritability, stress, and finally visual hallucinations. Such results might be correlated with behavior found in the sterile environment of some homes and classrooms.

The curiosity motive was demonstrated by the Salvatore Maddi experiment with nursery school children.[8]

In this study the element of novelty and the intensity, color, and complexity of the stimuli were found to be important variables that arouse interest of people. These elements might well be considered in the structuring of classroom activities.

In speaking of activity and manipulatory motives, Murray states, "a developing child is motivated to *do* things—to run, climb, throw, jump, hold, drop, open, and close."[9] Here the *physical* orientation of the young is also evident.

In Lee Bennett Hopkins' *Let Them Be Themselves,* which serves as a useful storehouse of ideas for language-arts enrichment activities, creative dramatics is presented as a means of facilitating language development and a readiness for reading:

> "Thinking, daydreaming, imagining, playing, doing, and acting are all components of the art of being somewhere, something, or

[7] Murray, Edward J.: *Motivation and Emotion.* Lazarus, Richard S. (Ed.): *Foundations of Psychology Series,* Englewood Cliffs, New Jersey, Prentice-Hall, Inc., 1964, p. 76.

[8] *Ibid.,* p. 76.

[9] *Ibid.,* p. 78.

someone else. In the earliest years children's play is filled with acting. The block corner in the nursery and kindergarten is the place where young boys instantly become grown-up men—putting out fires, constructing bridges, or being at war with an enemy. A doll corner is 'I am the Mommy. I'll take care of you, baby. I'll do the dishes and wash the floors and change your diapers and watch TV just like my Mommy.' "[10]

Hopkins goes on to state that "When children participate in dramatic play, they cooperate with one another, they begin to feel the need for exchanging ideas, they speak, they listen, their vocabularies improve, readiness for reading takes place, and pathways are opened to the direct teaching phases of written communication."[11]

Creative play enables children to bring the world of Cinderellas, ogres, knights, and cops and robbers to have personal meaning through physical activity as they walk, talk, move, and react as these characters in the various situations they find themselves in.[12]

In outlining a variety of reading activities for an instructional program, Russell included *"Creative activities growing out of reading* to extend enjoyment or to reinforce the larger ideas of a selection or unit through dramatization, drawing a meaning, playing a game, or expressing ideas in rhythms."[13]

In speaking of working with those children with reading problems, Strang states, "Successful teaching of retarded readers depends also on discovering what makes them tick."[14] Here we see the author's willingness to use the strengths and capacities of the child if the teacher is to affect a learning environment that will provide success for the child. Strang proceeds to summarize a broad view of reading:

"Every promising path to improvement in reading demands an understanding of both the reading process and the reader. Viewed

[10] Hopkins, Lee Bennett: *Let Them Be Themselves,* New York, Citation Press, 1969, p. 152.

[11] *Ibid.,* p. 153.

[12] *Ibid.*

[13] Russell, David H.: *Children Learn to Read,* 2nd ed. New York, Ginn and Company, 1961, p. 145.

[14] Strang, Ruth: *Diagnostic Teaching of Reading,* 2nd ed. New York, McGraw-Hill Book Company, 1969, p. 5.

as communication the reading process involves the abilities (1) to decode or decipher the author's printed words, (2) to associate them with meaning gained through the reader's firsthand experience and previous reading, and (3) to express the ideas thus acquired through speaking, drawing, writing, or other verbal or motor responses. The broad view of reading includes an understanding of what constitutes effective reading, what contributes to effective reading, and what interferes with effective reading."[15]

In an ESEA Title I project for oral language development of kindergarten and first grade children in the Syracuse City School System, action games along with experience stories and creative dramatics were activities used for providing drill in producing correct sounds. In the project the experimental group did significantly better than the control group when tested for oral communication skills. The increase in mean scores from the pre-test and post-test results was about eighteen points for the experimental group in contrast to an approximately nine-point gain in the control group.

And finally, two volumes that have had significant impact on those interested in and responsible for increasing opportunities for successful learning experiences for children also describe the shape of things to come, hopefully. Albert Cullum in *Push Back the Desks* describes vocabulary development activities for kindergarten that show how effective and stimulating a *physically*-oriented activity can be:

"One day I read to the children the poem, 'Fog' by Carl Sandburg and at the end I said, 'Now you sit on your haunches.'

"They couldn't fathom the word haunches, but as soon as I asked them to sit as a cat would sit, the magic circle of twenty-two became twenty-two cats sitting on their haunches. We all found it very comfortable sitting on our haunches.

"Another time I flapped and flapped my arms, sometimes slowly and calmly and other times frantically. They guessed correctly when they said I was a bird.

"But what about my arms that are always moving, sometimes slowly and sometimes swiftly? What are they called besides wings?

"Naturally they couldn't guess the word 'pinions,' but they accepted the word without batting an eyelash. Everyone used his pinions that day."[16]

[15] *Ibid.*
[16] Cullum, Albert: *Push Back the Desks.* New York, Citation Press, 1967, pp. 61–63.

The author goes on to describe the best day "when I was a huge wave and there were sandpipers pecking for food on the beach. They screamed and squealed as they avoided the splash of the big wave as they raced to safety by touching the blackboard." At the conclusion of Mr. Cullum's year of developing the vocabulary of twenty-two kindergarten children by sixty new words he devised a test to see how well they retained their big words: "Without any review, over 90 per cent of the class scored one hundred! The words were still alive."[17] Even if researchers might find weaknesses in the evaluation procedures and the results claimed, the most doubting reader would probably acknowledge those children did learn and retain words and they would accept the logic that *physically*-oriented activities facilitated this learning experience.

Charles E. Silberman's *Crisis in the Classroom* likewise has dramatically aroused the interest and concern of many about the need for remaking American education institutions and their instructional programs. Silberman, in Part III, "How Schools Should be Changed," describes informal education and the informal classroom whereby "the teacher is the facilitator rather than the source of learning, the source being the child himself."[18] The detailed description of the new English primary school program versus traditional programs of this section is pertinent to this text in terms of citing learning activities he considers to be the embodiment of his concepts of what educational experiences for children should be.

ITEM: A Learning Center teacher directs a first grade class in a series of games designed to show how different kinds of language—gestures, actions, words—can portray different moods, situations, identities.

> "Let's look angry in as many different ways as you can," she tells the children. "Now let's laugh in different ways," she says. "First let's giggle." "Now let's snicker." "Let me hear a belly laugh like Santa gives."

As groups of children make up their own variants, the teacher

[17] *Ibid.*, p. 65.

[18] Silberman, Charles E.: *Crisis in the Classroom.* New York, Random House, 1970, p. 268.

begins playing a subtler game with two or three children at a time. In this game the child must describe a toy or game or other object without naming it, listing as many characteristics as possible—size, shape, color, texture, etc.—until the teacher or another child can pick it off the shelf.[19]

ITEM: The teacher directs a group of children in a game about circles. The children dance into large circles, small circles, tiny circles. They intersect. They form concentric circles. Then with pencils, paper, and compasses the children each make a "Circle Book," no two of which are alike. It is clear that they understand terms like "connecting," "concentric," "intersecting," as well as subtle differences between "huge" and "large" or "small" and "tiny."[20]

Such learning activities for developing the concept of the circle may be contrasted with a series of suggested activities for kindergarten children from a current text in reading instruction. In the latter, recommended activities include: discussion of what a circle is, show and discuss objects in pictures and in the children's environment that are circular in shape, assemble bulletin board of pictures of circular objects that are labeled "circle," examine different size and color circles, paste cut-out circles on sheet of paper (in design if the children wish), show and discuss circle scrapbook prepared by teacher. Activities to help children begin to print letters comprised of circles include children tracing circles drawn on a dittoed sheet (making certain the children are using correct direction), making circles in the air and drawing their own circles on paper. The children begin to print the letter *o* and later *c*.

These recommended activities from this particular reading text are valid types of activities. But if the learning environment also included *physically*-oriented type activities described by Silberman to develop the concept of the circle, the learning experiences of these children would be enriched and based on sounder concepts of the learning process and child growth and development principles. It is not a matter of an *either-or* choice of method. It is rather that the reading instructional programs

[19] *Ibid.,* pp. 308–309.
[20] *Ibid.,* p. 309.

of our schools can be strengthened by adding the dimension of motor learning in classroom activities.

MEANING OF MOTOR LEARNING

The term "motor learning" has been defined in a number of ways. Most of these definitions are more alike than they are different, tending to center around the general idea that motor learning is concerned only with the learning of motor skills. As an example, the *Dictionary of Education* differentiates between what might be termed *ideational* learning and *motor* learning in the following manner: Ideational learning is concerned with ideas, concepts, and mental associations, while motor learning is that in which the learner achieves new facility in the performance of bodily movements as a result of specific practice.[21] Although this may be a convenient and simple description of motor learning, it does not serve the purpose adequately in modern times. The reason for this is that motor learning can no longer be considered a unilateral entity. At one time, when thought of only in terms of learning motor skills, it might have been considered by some as almost the exclusive purview of the physical educator and psychologist. However, it has now become such a multiphasic area that it compels the interest and attention of a variety of professions and disciplines.

Various aspects of motor learning in one way or another are involved in such fields as physical education, psychology, psychiatry, and neurophysiology. In fact, in almost any endeavor of human concern that one might mention, some aspect of motor learning could play a very significant part. It is for this reason that we no longer think of motor learning only in the sense of the previously mentioned definition. Consequently, some attempt needs to be made to identify certain branches of specific aspects of motor learning. This is the case with the present volume, *TEACHING READING THROUGH MOTOR LEARNING.*

[21] Good, Carter V.: *Dictionary of Education*, 2nd ed. New York, McGraw-Hill Book Co., Inc., p. 314, 1959.

Branches of Motor Learning

In order to put this particular topic into its proper perspective, and to establish a suitable frame of reference for subsequent discussions of it, we will identify three specific aspects of motor learning.[22] It should be understood that these identifications are used arbitrarily for our own purpose. Others may identify these differently, and in the absence of anything resembling standardized terminology, it is their prerogative to do so. Moreover, it is also recognized that some individuals might wish to segment these aspects of motor learning further, or add others. With this in mind we will identify the three aforementioned aspects as follows:

1. Motor learning which is concerned essentially with conditions surrounding the *learning of motor skills.*
2. Motor learning which is concerned essentially with *perceptual motor development.* (This may also be referred to as *psychomotor development* or *neuromotor perceptual training.*)
3. Motor learning which is concerned essentially with *academic skill and concept development.*

It should be clearly understood that all of the above areas of motor learning involve the same general basic concept; and that there are various degrees of interrelatedness and interdependence of each area upon the other.

Motor Learning Involving the Learning of Motor Skills

This branch of motor learning has commanded the attention of individuals in the field of physical education mainly because it forms the basic citadel for subject matter and methods of teaching in this field. Some of the areas in which attention has been centered include: how individuals learn motor skills, length and distribution of practice, mechanical principles, transfer, and retention. Research in some of these areas by some physical edu-

[22] To our knowledge this particular classification of motor learning was first introduced into the literature as follows: Humphrey, James H.: Academic skill and concept development through motor activity. *The Academy Papers,* No. 1, The American Academy of Physical Education, pp. 29–35, 1968.

cators has been outstanding, and, as might be expected it has been done primarily by those who have some background in psychology.

In recent years it appears that there has been more compatibility between psychologists and physical educators regarding this branch of motor learning. The fact that such has not always been the case is suggested in the following comment by one psychologist.[23]

> "There is one perhaps distressing feature which is apparent: this is the seeming lack of awareness which the two disciplines have of the progress *and* problems of the other's area."

Fortunately there is evidence of amelioration of this condition because more and more, psychologists are discovering that physical education and sports experiences provide an excellent natural climate and laboratory for the study of human performance and behavior. We should mention again that this aspect was the only subject of definition of motor learning in the *Dictionary of Education.* Moreover, it will *not* be the function of the present text to deal with this branch of motor learning as such. There are a number of fine books devoted entirely to this branch of motor learning which may be found in most major libraries.

Motor Learning Involving Perceptual Motor Development

This branch of motor learning involves the correction, or at least some degree of improvement, of certain motor deficiencies, especially those associated with fine coordinations. An example of the need for this type of training may be seen with certain neurologically handicapped children who may have various types of learning disorders. What some specialists have identified as a "perceptual-motor-deficit" syndrome is said to exist in such cases. An attempt may be made to correct or improve fine motor control problems through a carefully developed sequence of motor competencies, which follow a definite hierarchy of development. This may occur through either structured or unstructured programs, some representative examples of which will be

---

[23] Johnson, G.B.: Motor learning. In W.R. Johnson (Ed.): *Science and Medicine of Exercise and Sports.* New York, Harper and Brothers, p. 602, 1960.

discussed in a subsequent chapter. (As far as physical education is concerned, this branch of motor learning might well be
thought of as learning *of* the physical.)

In recent years various aspects of this area of motor learning
have contributed to the alleviation of certain types of learning
disorders in children. It should be apparent that a wide range of
specialists and disciplines are needed to help children effectively
through this area of motor learning. We previously called attention to certain areas of specialty which in one way or another
can make important contributions. It will be a part of the function of this volume to explore this dimension of motor learning as
it is concerned with the specific area of reading, and a subsequent
chapter will be devoted entirely to this aspect.

Motor Learning Involving Academic Skill and Concept Development Through Motor Activity

This might also be referred to as the "physical education learning medium." This branch of motor learning is concerned specifically with children learning basic skills and concepts in various
subject areas in the elementary school curriculum through the
medium of motor activity. (Whereas motor learning involving
perceptual motor development was thought of in terms of learning *of* the physical, this aspect of motor learning is concerned
with learning *through* the physical.) The primary focus and purpose of the present volume will be on the contribution this aspect
of motor learning can make to reading.

It may be interesting to note that one well-known psychologist, Dr. James J. Asher, has identified this branch of motor learning as, "total physical response motor learning."[24] Asher suggests
that research in motor learning is usually done with tasks which
involve *parts* of the body—the receptors and effectors—as illus-
trated in display-control problems, rather than with the whole
body. His work with the total physical response technique has
been done in the area of learning foreign language and essentially involves having students listen to a command in a foreign
language and immediately respond with the appropriate phys-

[24] Asher, James J.: The total physical response technique of learning. *Journal
of Special Education*, Fall, 1969.

ical action. In connection with our work, Asher comments as follows:

> "The work that comes closest to total physical response motor learning is Humphrey's investigations of learning through games in which, for example, the acquisition of certain reading skills was significantly accelerated when the learning task occurred in the context of a game involving the entire body."

The idea of motor activity learning is not new. In fact, the application of motor activity was a basic principle of the Froebelian kindergarten and was based on the theory that children learn and acquire information, understanding, and skills through motor activities in which they are naturally interested, such as building, constructing, modeling, painting and various forms of movement.

When we speak of motor activity learning in the present text we refer to things that children *do* actively in a pleasurable situation in order to learn. This should suggest to classroom teachers that motor learning activities can be derived from basic physical education curriculum content found in such broad categories as *game* activities, *rhythmic* activities, and *self-testing* activities. Hence, our reason for indicating previously that learning through motor activity can also be referred to as the physical education learning medium. Classroom teachers and physical education teachers might well team up to facilitate learning and development of skills in their respective areas of responsibility through an integrated and cross-reinforcement program.

This aspect of motor learning is based essentially on the theory that children—being predominantly movement oriented—will learn better when what we will arbitrarily call "academic learning" takes place through pleasurable physical activity; that is, when the *motor* component operates at a maximal level in skill and concept development in school subject areas essentially oriented to so-called "verbal" learning. This is *not* to say that "motor" and "verbal" learning are two mutually exclusive kinds of learning, although it has been suggested that at the two extremes the dichotomy appears justifiable. It is recognized that in verbal learning which involves almost complete abstract symbolic manipulations there may be among others, such motor components as tension, subvocal speech, and physiological changes in metabolism which operate at a minimal level. It is also recognized that in physical education activities where the learning is predominantly motor in nature, verbal learning is evident, although perhaps at a minimal level. For example, in teaching a physical education activity there is a certain amount of verbalization in developing a kinesthetic concept of the particular activity that is being taught.

One way to use motor activity learning involves the selection of a physical education activity which is taught to children and used as a learning activity for the development of a skill or concept in a specific subject area. An attempt is made to arrange an *active* learning situation so that a fundamental intellectual skill or concept is being acted out, practiced, or rehearsed in the course of participating in the physical education activity. By way of illustration, let us consider such an active learning situation which involves the reading skill: *To distinguish between words that use the "c" or "s" in making the "s" sound.* The motor activity learning experience to develop the skill is a game called "C's" and "S's" which is an adaptation of the game *Crows and Cranes* as shown in the following diagram:

```
|                    C    S                    |
|                    C    S                    |
|                    C    S                    |
|                    C    S                    |
|                    C    S                    |
|                    C    S                    |
|                    C    S                    |
|                    C    S                    |
Goal                                        Goal
```

The children are divided equally into two groups, the "C's" and the "S's" who line up facing each other, with their lines about five feet apart. A goal line is drawn a given distance behind each group. The teacher calls out a word that is spelled with either a "c" or an "s." If the word requires a "c," all of the "C's" run to reach their goal line before being tagged by a member of the "S's" group. All of those tagged become members of the opposite group. The groups then return to their respective lines and the same procedure is followed with another word. The group having the greater number of players on its side at the end of a specified playing time is the winner.

This particular motor activity learning situation was used and compared with a traditional learning activity as follows: A standard language workbook exercise was used and this consisted of a list of 12 words containing both "c" and "s" sounds. In the exercise there were questions concerning which letters spelled the "c" or "s" sounds. In addition, this exercise required that the children write the words that used the "c" or "s" sounds.

Twenty third grade children were pretested on the skill and divided into two groups on the basis of their scores. Both groups were taught by the same teacher and with one group the motor learning activity was used and with the other group the traditional language workbook exercise was used to develop the reading skill. A posttest showed that the motor activity group made a gain of 13 per cent while the traditional group made a gain of 7 per cent. There was a difference in per cent of gain of 54 per cent in favor of the motor-activity group. These data were extracted from the original study which will be dealt with in greater detail in the following chapter.

The intent of the preceding discussions has been to clarify the authors' concept of motor learning. And further, to help the reader gain insight into some of the possibilities of the motor learning activity medium.

CHAPTER TWO

THEORETICAL PERSPECTIVES

THE CONCEPT OF TOTAL PERSONALITY
IN CHILD GROWTH AND DEVELOPMENT

G ENERALLY SPEAKING, total growth and development is the fundamental purpose of the education of children. All attempts at such education should take into account a combination of physical, social, emotional, as well as intellectual aspects of human behavior. A great deal of clinical and experimental evidence indicates that a human being must be considered as a whole and not a collection of parts. For our purpose here we would prefer to use the term "total personality" in referring to the child as a unified individual or total being. Perhaps a more common term used in connection with children of elementary school age is the "whole child." The term total personality, however, is commonly used in the fields of mental health and psychology and recently has been gaining more usage in the field of education. Moreover, when we consider it from a point of man existing as a person, it is interesting to note that "existence as a person" is one rather common definition of personality.

What then comprises the total personality? Anyone who has difficulty in formulating his views with regard to what the human personality actually consists of can take courage in the knowledge that many experts who spend their time studying it are not always in complete agreement as to what it is or how it operates. Indeed, one of the greatest mysteries which confronts man in our modern society is man himself. If one were to analyze the literature on the subject he would find generally

19

that the total personality consists of the sum of all the physical, social, emotional, and intellectual aspects—both historical and current of any individual. The personality is *one thing,* though admittedly complex in nature and never static, comprising these various major aspects. These components are highly interrelated and interdependent. The condition of any one aspect affects each other aspect to a degree and, hence the personality as a whole. The total personality, to be in a healthy state, must have balance and health in each area.

When a nervous child stutters or becomes nauseated, a mental state is *not* directly causing a physical symptom. On the contrary, a pressure imposed upon the organism causes a series of reactions which include thought, verbalization, digestive processes, and muscular function. Mind does not cause the body to become upset; the total organism is upset by a situation and reflects its upset in several ways, including disturbances in thought, feeling, and bodily processes. The whole individual responds in interaction with the social and physical environment. And, as the individual is affected by his environment, he, in turn, has an effect upon it.

However, because of long tradition during which physical development and intellectual development have been separate entities in the curriculum and receiving different emphasis, we are still accustomed to dividing the two in our thinking and their placement within our value system. The result may be that we sometimes pull human beings apart with this kind of thinking. And evidence is being gathered to support the notion that we are not using physical development and motor learning as we might to serve our efforts to reach the objective of the development of the total personality.

Traditional attitudes which separate the mind and body tend to lead to unbalanced development of the child with respect to mind and body and/or social adjustment. What is more important is that we fail to utilize the strengths of one to serve the needs of the other. To understand better the concept of total personality the human organism can be seen in terms of the diagram in Figure 1.

The circle is the total environment of the individual which

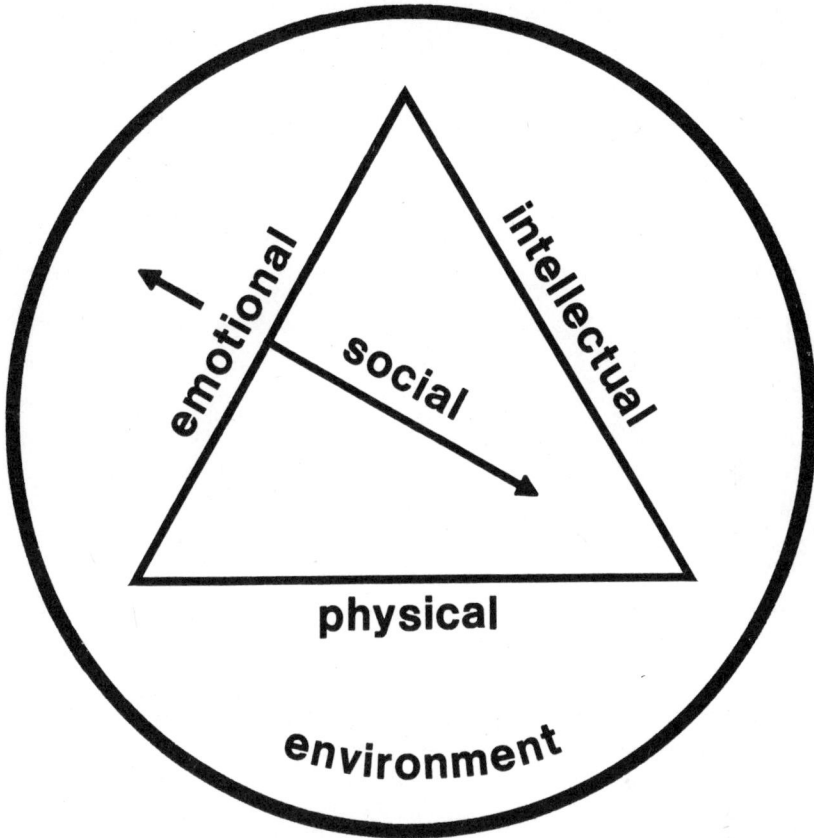

Figure 1. Schematic Diagram of "Total Personality."

circumscribes and confines all aspects of the total personality. The triangle with its three sides—physical, emotional, and intellectual aspects of the total personality—form a single figure with the *physical* as a base. An arrow extending from the center of the triangle upward through one of the sides, is designated *social* to represent interpersonal relationships within the field of the individual and his environment. The arrow is pointed at both ends to suggest a two-way process: the individual is affected by those around him, and he affects them (largely through language as his means of communication). The triangle is dependent upon a balance of all its parts, and if one part of the triangle is changed the entire triangle is reshaped. It is interesting to draw diagrams in which one after the other of the sides is shortened—as in one kind or another of developmental failure or retardation—and see how this affects the triangle. It is also interesting to make personal applications such as the following: "What happens to my intellectual performance when I am worried or have a stomach ache?" "What changes occur in my body when I 'feel' frightened, embarrassed, or angered?" Obviously, similar applications can be made to children.

It is interesting that in this day, when great emphasis is placed upon social adjustment, that perhaps our major problems involve faulty interpersonal relationships. For this reason it is important to make special note of the interaction between the individual and his environment. The quality of the individual's interpersonal relationships affect all the other aspects of his personality. How well do you drive when someone is shouting at you? How well can you concentrate when you think someone is talking about you? These are social circumstances which affect the physical, intellectual, and emotional organism. We also know the devastation of self-concept from our educational evaluation system and the resulting number of school dropouts.

But this matter of interpersonal relationships is still more fundamental to growth and development than the foregoing illustration suggests. For example, it has been found that infants and very young children who are deprived of a reasonable amount of mothering—that initial and basic social experience—actually stop growing in one or more aspects of their personality, even though all of their other needs are met. Thus, some fail to develop mentally. Some show both physical immaturity and mental retardation. Still others are affected mainly at the emotional level. That is, if they are deprived of love and given, instead, nonloving care, they may fail to grow emotionally and not be capable of human feeling as we generally think of it. This may be the cause of the so-called psychopathic personality, that most unfeeling, antisocial, "wolf in the fold" of criminal types. In brief, the quality of interpersonal relationships in the early years may tend to set the pattern of subsequent attitudes and behavior toward other people, authority, and the "rules of the game" of life generally.

The subject of language development deserves special comment as an aspect of social interaction. The infant's first social contact is by way of his skin, as he is fed, fondled and caressed. This communication via the skin expresses the warm relationship between mother and child and is a kind of "language of the body" which both understand deeply and which will linger throughout life as a fundamental way of "expressing" love and affection. But as the child develops intellectually, language replaces touch as the prime medium of social interaction. Gradually, language in spoken and written form becomes a major influence in the child's environment. In recent years the implications of the quantity and quality of language has been given increasing recognition for the growth and development of the total personality of the child. For example, in some homes mealtime is a time of gossip, a period of criticizing and ridiculing friends, neighbors, fellow workers, and so on. Or perhaps worse, it is a time of intrafamily verbal conflict. Not only is such talk and the model that it constitutes in the child's mind of questionable value from a social health point of view, but also the aroused emotions are likely to affect digestion adversely and to establish certain deep-seated attitudes regarding eating and meals.

All of these things then are the basis of total personality—a complex balance of psychophysical and social considerations which prepare the individual for the fullest, most socially valuable, productive and adventuresome living. Childhood is the time when attitudes and patterns of living are established, and it is therefore of urgent importance that parents and educators concern themselves with meeting the total personality needs of children.

THE PHYSICAL ASPECT OF PERSONALITY

In view of the fact that this text is primarily concerned with human physical movement as a way of learning we need to direct specific attention to the physical aspect of personality.

One point of departure in discussing the physical aspect of personality could be to state that "everybody has a body." Some are short, some are tall, some are lean, and some are fat. Children come in different sizes, but all of them have a certain innate physical capacity which is influenced by the environment.

It might be said of the child that he *is* his body. It is something he can see. It is his base of operation—what we referred to as the *physical base* in the triangle of total personality. The other components of the total personality—social, emotional and intellectual—are somewhat vague as far as the child is concerned. Although these are manifested in various ways, the child does not actually see them as he does the physical aspect. Consequently, it becomes all important that the child be helped early in life to gain control over the physical aspect, or what is known as basic body control. This in turn will aid him in terms of a positive body image and hence, a better understanding of himself which will aid him in his attempts to control his environment. The ability to gain basic body control will of course vary from one child to another. It will depend upon such components of physical fitness as strength, endurance, coordination, agility and others that might be considered as elements of physical fitness of the human organism.

In earlier eras of human existence, education was primarily a matter of developing physical skills and prowess because survival, and success in life depended heavily upon a man's might and endurance. Education in these times also focused on developing man's beliefs and commitment though not necessarily through literacy by which he might establish his own value system.

Today a man's success depends increasingly upon other skills, such as those with relatively small muscle responses (such as those of hands, eyes, and vocal cords), and upon the more complex cognitive processes of abstract thinking. Consequently, education has concerned itself mainly with developing these skills with particular emphasis upon the manipulating of symbols such as words and numbers. Meanwhile, education of the physical aspect of the total personality has been assigned a minor role in the general education processes of this nation. Upon first consideration this might seem reasonable until we stop to consider the violence that it does in terms of the biological heritage of man and the nature of children.

Traditional thinking, as we have noted earlier, has tended to bring about a separation of mind and body, with the result that physical fitness is commonly considered an isolated quality of the individual and having no special relationship with other aspects of the personality. Thinking back again to the triangular representation of the human personality, however, we are reminded that the physical aspect is an integral, and perhaps as far as the child is concerned, the most important part of the total organism.

Ample and worthwhile physical activity tends to guarantee that the child will develop a solid base from which to operate in the course of his progress in the developmental and educational processes. Moreover, it may be said that the ultimate source of the individual's belief that he can exercise control over his environment is his knowledge that he can control himself, his body and his movements. When children are unable to control their movements and those bodily functions which are ordinarily under volitional control, they have little or no basis for believing that they can exercise control over anything external to them. It is for this reason that numerous children who are deficient in all or even some of the usual activities expected of children suddenly spring into the range of "normal" when their physical base is improved. It is encouraging to note, however, that there is widespread dissatisfaction among laymen and those interested in facilitating human growth and learning regarding the increasing percentages of humans not achieving at their level of potential, and that researchers and practitioners of all disciplines are looking for ways to affect more positively growth and development of our human resources. It is also encouraging to note that in very recent years there has been a growing awareness of the importance of physical development *and* the utilizing of motor learning in the educative process, not only for school-age children, but for preschool children as well.

MOVEMENT

One of the most fundamental characteristics of life is movement. Whatever else they may involve, all of man's achievements are based upon his ability to move. Obviously, the very young child is not an intelligent being in the sense of performing abstract thinking, and he only gradually acquires the ability to deal with symbols and intellectualize his experiences in the course of his development. On the other hand, the child is a creature of movement and feeling. Any efforts to educate the child must take this relative dominance of the intellectual versus movement and feeling into account. Furthermore, by engaging in movement experiences to develop academic skills and concepts, these skills and concepts become a part of the child's physical reality. This involves *proprioception* or muscle sense.

The systems of perception, or sensory processes as they are sometimes referred to, are ordinarily considered to consist of the senses of sight, hearing, touch, smell and taste. Armington has suggested that although this point of view is convenient for some purposes, it greatly oversimplifies the ways by which information can be fed into the human organism.[1] He indicates also that a number of sources of sensory input are overlooked, particularly the senses that enable the body to maintain its correct posture. As a matter of fact, the sixty to seventy pounds of muscle which include over six hundred in number that are attached to the skeleton of the averaged-sized man could well be his most important sense organ.

Various estimates indicate that the visual sense brings us upwards of three-fourths of our knowledge. Therefore, it could be said with little reservation that man is eye-minded. However, Steinhaus has reported that a larger portion of the nervous system is devoted to receiving and integrating sensory input originating in the muscles and joint structures than is devoted to the eye and ear combined.[2] In view of this Steinhaus also contends that man is *muscle-sense* minded.

[1] Armington, John C.: *Physiological Basis of Psychology.* Dubuque, Iowa, William C. Brown Co., 1966, p. 16.

[2] Steinhaus, Arthur H: Your muscles see more than your eyes. *Journal of Health, Physical Education and Recreation,* 37:38, September, 1966.

As mentioned above, proprioception is concerned with muscle sense. The proprioceptors are sensory nerve terminals that give information concerning movements and position of the body. A proprioceptive feedback mechanism is involved, which in a sense regulates movement. In view of the fact that children are so movement oriented, it appears a reasonable speculation that proprioceptive feedback from the receptors of muscles, skin and joints can contribute in a facilitative manner in the development of reading skills and concepts. In addition it is well known by experienced classroom teachers at the primary grade levels that the child's motor mechanism is active to the extent that it is almost an impossibility for him to remain in a quiet state for a very long time regardless of the passiveness of the learning situation. To demand prolonged sedentary states of young children is actually, in a sense, in defiance of a basic physiological principle. This is concerned directly with the child's basal metabolism. The basal metabolic rate is indicative of the speed at which body fuel is changed to energy, as well as how fast this energy is used.

Basal metabolic rate can be measured in terms of calories per meter of body surface, with a calorie representing a unit measure of heat energy in food. It has been found that on the average, basal metabolism rises from birth to about two or three years of age, at which time it starts to decline until between the ages of twenty to twenty-four. Also the rate is higher for boys than for girls. With the highest metabolic rate, and therefore the greatest amount of energy available during the early school years, deep consideration might well be given to learning activities through which this energy can be utilized. Moreover, it has been observed that there is an increased attention span of primary-age children during active play. When a task such as a motor learning activity is meaningful to a child, he can spend longer periods engaged in it than is likely to be the case in some of the more traditional sedentary types of learning activities.

The foregoing discussions have attempted to take into account various basic principles of child growth and development that are compatible with child learning. It is the hope of the authors that the present volume will help the reader to take

advantage of some of these principles particularly as they relate to motor learning.[3] In sum, emphasis has been placed upon
the idea that children will grow and develop in their reading
when the learning that takes place in a pleasurable active situation as a part of their physical reality replaces and/or supple-
ments traditional abstract learning situations.

SOME EVIDENCE IN SUPPORT OF THE THEORY

It was mentioned before that the concept of motor-activity
learning is not new. Throughout the ages the idea has been
held in high esteem by many outstanding philosophers and
educators. Such pronouncements extend over several centuries
from Plato's assertion that "learning takes place best through
play and play situations" to a modern twentieth century statement by L.P. Jacks that "the discovery of the educational possibilities of the play side of life may be counted one of the greatest discoveries of the present day." In the specific area of reading, as far back as the seventeenth century Fénelon is reputed
to have said that he had seen certain children who had learned
to read while playing. The favorable comments of such people
obviously carry a great deal of weight. However, in an age
when so much emphasis is placed upon scientific inquiry and
research we cannot and should not rely only on the subjective
opinion of even some of the most highly regarded thinkers in
history. Thus, the need for some supporting evidence.

There are many ways of studying how behavioral changes
take place in children, and various techniques in studying the
phenomenon of learning about the various facets of reading
through motor learning are reflected in the reports that follow.

The first study reported here was one of an exploratory
nature and involved the integration of physical education ac-

---

[3] The reader may be interested in the following books which also emphasize
this general approach: Humphrey, James H., and Sullivan, Dorothy D.: *Teaching
Slow Learners Through Active Games.* Springfield, Illinois, Charles C Thomas,
Publisher, 1970 and Humphrey, James H.: *Child Learning Through Elementary
School Physical Education.* Dubuque, Iowa, William C. Brown Publishers, 1966.

tivities and reading vocabulary.[4] The main purpose of the study was to attempt to find out how participation in physical education activities affected the reading vocabulary of a selected group of third grade children. The assumption was that if words taken up in reading are integrated with physical education lessons, children would more readily learn the words because of their inherent interest in active play.

The procedure used involved equating two groups of subjects according to their scores on the *California Test of Mental Maturity, S-Form,* the Reading Vocabulary Test from the *California Achievement Battery,* and according to their reading group level. Thirty subjects were equated into two groups on this basis. There were four reading group levels represented within each group of 15 subjects in the experimental group (vocabulary words integrated with physical education lessons).

The subjects in both groups were given a reading vocabulary test at the beginning and the end of the two-week experimental period on words that were used from their reader in the experiment. Both the experimental and control groups had the same reading and physical education lessons; the experimental group had one variable involved. In this group the teacher attempted to integrate words used in the experiment as a part of the physical education lessons.

There were no statistically significant differences for the different reading groups or between the experimental and control groups. However, some interesting observations were made on the basis of percentage of gain and/or loss of subjects in both the experimental and control groups. Of the entire group, 73.3 per cent of the subjects in the experimental group improved on the second vocabulary test, while 46.6 per cent of the control group improved on the second test. An obvious weakness of the study was the fact that the groups were taught by different

[4] Humphrey, James H., and Link, Ruth B.: An exploratory study of integration of physical education activities and reading vocabulary with selected third grade children. Proceedings of the Research Section, American Association for Health, Physical Education and Recreation (Portland, Oregon, March 1959), Washington, D.C.

teachers, although both teachers were classified as outstanding by their superiors.

In a pilot study using the single group experimental proce-dure the purpose was to explore the extent to which third grade children can develop certain language arts concepts through the medium of active game participation.[5]

Twenty-three third-grade children were pretested on eight language arts concepts which were to be taken up as a part of their regular class work during the ensuing two weeks. Eight active games in which the eight language arts concepts were inherent, and which were appropriate for use at the third-grade level, were selected. These games were taught to the children over a two-week period and used as learning media for the de-velopment of the language arts concepts. The children were retested after the active game medium was used. In every case there was a gain in the raw scores between the first and second test. A statistical comparison between the scores of the tests before and after use of the active games to develop the language arts concepts indicated learning at .01 level of significance.

Subjective evaluations were also made with regard to teacher-pupil reaction. This was done for the purpose of collecting information which would not be likely to show up in a statisti-cal analysis, and yet which might be of considerable importance in pointing up certain trends.

As expected, there was a highly positive reaction from the children in favor of this approach to learning, and it was their general feeling that all learning experiences should take place in this manner. A subjective evaluation by the cooperating teacher yielded the following interesting generalizations: First, that the motivational nature of the physical education learning medium not only facilitated learning, but teaching as well. Sec-ond, that some concepts could be developed better through the physical education learning medium than any other teaching

[5] Humphrey, James H.: The use of physical education as a learning medium in the development of language arts concepts in third-grade children. *Research Quarterly*, Washington, D.C., March 1962.

procedure known to the teacher. (This observation was particularly important in that the cooperating teacher was a language arts specialist.) And third, that better retention of concepts was noted when this procedure was used in comparison with other procedures used with other third grade children. This possibility was suggested after casual oral questioning of several children at various intervals of time after the study had been completed.

In a follow up of the above study the parallel group experimental procedure was used.[6] Twenty third-grade children were equated into two groups on the basis of pretest scores on ten language understandings. One group was taught through the active-game medium and the other group was taught through traditional language workbooks. Both groups had the same teacher. Comparisons were made of the pretest and post-test scores of the language workbook group and also the active game group. The statistical analysis showed that both groups learned, but that the active-game group learned at a higher level of significance. When the post-test scores of both groups were analyzed, it was indicated that the active-game group learned significantly more than the language workbook group.

In recognition of the limitations imposed by a study of this nature, it was concluded that if one accepts the significant differences in the tests scores as evidence of learning, these third-grade children could develop language comprehension through both active games and the traditional language workbook medium, although the active game group produced greater changes.

The next experiment reported here involved a detailed study of the reactions of six- to eight-year-old children when reading material is oriented to active game participation.[7] This experiment was initiated on the premise of relating reading content for six- to eight-year old children to their natural urge to play.

---

[6] Humphrey, James H.: Comparison of the use of active games and language workbook exercises as learning media in the development of language understandings with third grade children. *Perceptual and Motor Skills, 21*:23, 1965.

[7] Humphrey, James H., and Moore, Virginia D.: Improving reading through physical education. *Education,* (The Reading Issue), May 1960, p. 559.

Ten Games were written with a story setting that described how to play the games.[8] (In a subsequent chapter entitled, "Motor Oriented Reading Content," detailed information will be provided for the reader with reference on how to prepare his or her own original stories.) The manuscripts were very carefully prepared. Care was given to the reading values and the literary merits of each story. Attention was focused upon: (1) particular reading skills; (2) concept development; (3) vocabulary load, that is, in terms of the number, repetition and difficulty of words; and (4) length, phrasing, and number of sentences per story.

When the manuscripts were prepared the *New Readability Formula for Grades I-III* by George D. Spache was applied to judge the reading difficulty of the material. Application of this formula revealed results shown in Table I.

A total of 968 words was used in the stories. Eleven of these words, or about 1 per cent were *not* included in the *Clarence H. Stone's Revision of the Dale List of 769 Easy Words*, the word list used in the Spache Formula.

Thirty teachers in rural, suburban and city school systems working with 54 reading groups of children used and evaluated the stories in actual classroom situations. The reading groups varied in: (1) number, from 3 to 33; (2) chronological age, from 5 years 9 months to 9 years 8 months; (3) intelligence

TABLE I

READING DIFFICULTY OF THE GAME STORIES
BASED ON THE SPACHE FORMULA

Factors Inherent in the Stories	Range	Median	Mean
Number of Words Per Story	56–143	103.5	96.8
Number of Sentences Per Story	8–24	15.5	15.6
Number of Words Per Sentence	4.9–7.1	6.5	6.2
Grade Level of Readability	1.6–2.2	1.85	1.85

[8] Additional stories were written (131 in all) and developed into a series of six books for first and second grade children. These books were published as the *Read and Play* Series by Garrard Publishing Company, Champaign, Illinois, 1962 and by Frederick Muller, Ltd., Ludgate House, 110 Fleet Street, London, E.C. 4, England, 1965.

quotient, from 52 to 136; and (4) grade placement, from first grade through third grade. The children represented to a reasonable extent a cross section of an average population with respect to ethnic background, socioeconomic level and the like. In all, 503 children read from one to three stories for a total of 1,007 different readings.

On report sheets especially designed for the purpose the teachers were asked to record observable evidence of certain comprehension skills being practiced by the reading groups before, during and after the children played the games they read about. The teachers were requested to make their evaluations on a comparative basis with other materials that had been read by the children. The results of these observations are shown in Table II.

The observations of the teachers indicated that the game stories gave the children opportunities to practice and maintain skills necessary for intelligent reading. While enriching and extending their experiences the children improved their general ability to read independently and "on their own."

In another dimension of the study teachers were asked to rate the degree of *interest* of the children in the reading on an arbitrary 5-point scale as follows: extreme interest, considerable interest, moderate interest, some interest, or little or no interest.

The fact that there was sustained interest in the game stories is shown in Table III. (The 25 cases in the last two categories involved children with intelligence quotients far below normal.)

TABLE II

COMPREHENSION SKILLS PRACTICED BY CHILDREN
AS OBSERVED BY TEACHERS

Comprehension Skill	Number of Groups Observed	Number and % of Groups Practicing Skills
Following Directions	54	49–91%
Noting and Using Sequence of Ideas	54	41–76%
Selecting Main Idea	54	41–76%
Getting Facts	54	36–67%
Organizing Ideas	54	25–46%
Building Meaningful Vocabulary	54	22–41%
Gaining Independence in Word Mastery	54	19–35%

TABLE III

DEGREE OF INTEREST IN THE READING AS RATED BY TEACHERS

Degree of Interest	Number and Per Cent of Cases
Extreme Interest	469–46%
Considerable Interest	242–24%
Moderate Interest	271–27%
Some Interest	22–2.7%
Little or No Interest	3– .3%

The results shown in Table III become more meaningful when it is considered that many of the classroom teachers reported that untold numbers of children sit in school and read with little or no interest. This dimension of the study tended to verify that reading is an active rather than a passive process. Apparently the children had a real and genuine purpose for reading. To satisfy their natural urge to play they were interested and read to learn how to play a new game.

The 30 participating teachers in this study expressed a great deal of interest as a result of their observations. In fact, some seemed to view the procedure as a possible panacea for most of the reading problems that occur in the school situation. However, the authors would be far more cautious in drawing conclusions from the results of this study. Nonetheless, on the basis of the findings and with the limitations involved in conducting such an experiment, the following tentative conclusions appear warranted:

1. When a child is self-motivated and interested, he reads. In this case the reading was done without motivating devices such as picture clues and illustrations. (However, the published materials resulting from this study alluded to in footnote 8 do include colorful illustrations that accompany each story.)

2. These game stories were found to be extremely successful in stimulating interest in reading and at the same time improving the child's ability to read.

3. Because the material for these game stories was scientifically selected, prepared and tested it is unique in the field

of children's independent reading material. The outcomes were most satisfactory in terms of children's interest in reading content of this nature.

The final study reported here was designed to evaluate the effectiveness of active games as a means of reinforcing reading skills with fourth-grade children.[9] The parallel experimental procedure was employed and the purpose of the study was to determine how well certain reading skills could be reinforced by the active game medium as compared with some of the traditional ways of reinforcing these skills. Perhaps it might be well at this point to consider the compatibility of motor-activity learning with *reinforcement theory*. Generally speaking, reinforcement might be described as an increase in the efficiency of a response to a stimulus brought about by the concurrent action of another stimulus. The basis for contending that the motor-activity learning medium is consistent with general reinforcement theory is that this medium reinforces attention to the learning task and learning behavior. It keeps children involved in the learning activity, which is perhaps the major area of application for reinforcement procedures.

In this study, 73 fourth-grade children were pretested on eight reading skills. Thirty of these children were divided into two groups. One group of 15 was designated as the active game group and the other group of 15 as the traditional or conventional group. Each reading skill was introduced and presented verbally to the two groups together. The groups were then separated, and with one group the reading skills were reinforced through various forms of active games. With the other group the reading skills were reinforced by such traditional media as a language workbook, dictionary, and prepared ditto sheets. Both groups were taught by the same teacher. The types of reading skills used in the study were word recognition, phonics, structural analysis, and vocabulary development. The following is an example of how one reading skill was reinforced

[9] Humphrey, James H.: The use of the active game learning medium in the reinforcement of reading skills with fourth grade children. *The Journal of Special Education*, 1:369, 1967.

with the active group: A phonics skill, *auditory perception of long and short vowels,* was reinforced in an adaptation of the game Steal the Bacon, as shown in the following diagram:

Team A		Team B
ā		u
ē		o
ī		i
ō		e
ū		a
a	Bacon	ū
e		ō
i		ī
o		ē
u		ā

Two teams face each other about 15 feet apart. An object (the bacon) is placed in the middle of the space between the two lines. The members of both teams are given like vowels, some with a short sound and some with a long sound. The teacher calls out a word with a short vowel, such as *flash, hit,* or *bet,* or a word containing a long vowel, such as *rode, wave,* or *shade.* The two children on each team who have the correct vowel sound run out and try to grab the object and return it to their line. If the player does so, his team scores two points, and if he is tagged by his opponent in the process, the opposing team scores one point. For example, if the teacher calls the word "cave," the child with the long ā on one team and the child with the long ā on the other team would try to retrieve the object. The children exchanged vowel sounds periodically.

After the reading skills were presented and reinforced in the manner described, both groups were retested. The experiment covered ten school days, allowing one day for pretesting, eight days for the experiment and a final day for post-testing. A statistical analysis was made of the pre- and post-test scores.

The range of scores on the pretest (80 items) was 42 to 70 with a mean of 57. The post-test scores for the active game group ranged from 54 to 76 with a mean of 69. The post-test scores for the traditional group ranged from 43 to 72 with a mean of 62. In 14 of 15 cases the child in the active game group scored higher on the post-test than did his counterpart in the traditional group. When comparing the mean scores statistically it was indicated that the active game group learned significantly more than the traditional group. If the significant differences in the test scores can be accepted as evidence of learning, it can then be said that the kinds of reading skills used in this study could be reinforced better by the active game learning medium than by some of the traditional approaches.

The highly positive results of this study give rise to some interesting speculations. It would appear that the active game learning approach established a more effective situation for learning reinforcement for the following reasons. First, the greater motivation of the children in the active game learning group meant accentuation of those behaviors directly pertinent to their learning activities, making these salient for the purpose of reinforcement. The *proprioceptive* emphasis in active game learning no doubt meant that a greater number of "responses" were associated with and conditioned to learning stimuli. Finally, the gratifying aspects of active play situations provided a generalized situation of "reinforcers."

SOME GENERALIZATIONS

In view of the fact that there are now some objective data to support a long-held hypothetical postulation, perhaps some generalized assumptions along with some reasonable speculations can be set forth with at least a degree of confidence. Obviously, the data reported in the foregoing studies are not extensive enough to carve out a clear-cut profile with regard to learning about the various facets of reading through motor learning. However, they are suggestive enough to give rise to some interesting generalizations which may be briefly summarized as follows:

1. The motor-activity approach results in positive attitudes of children toward learning-to-read activities.
2. Children tend to learn certain reading-oriented language arts skills as word recognition, phonics, and structural analysis better through motor-activity learning than through many of the traditional media.

3. Motor-oriented reading content has been found to be successful in stimulating children's sustained interest in reading while at the same time developing and reinforcing reading skills.
4. This approach appears to be more favorable for children with normal and below-normal intelligence.

Furthermore, more informal field testing and observation of classroom and clinic activities provides a basis for supporting some reasonable speculations of a further role of motor-activity learning:

1. In general, children tend to learn certain comprehension skills needed for success in reading better through motor-activity learning than through many of the traditional instructional approaches.
2. Motor learning activities appear to be better suited for diagnosing reading readiness and in some cases reading disability, than traditional diagnostic measures.
3. The motor-activity learning approach provides specific reinforcement essential to learning.

It will remain the responsibility of research in these areas to provide the conclusive evidence to support these speculations. There is hope, however, based on actual experience with this approach in the activities described in Chapters Five through Eight, to encourage those responsible for facilitating children learning to read to use this approach and to join in collecting evidence to verify the contribution of motor-activity learning to the educational curriculum.

CHAPTER THREE

MOTOR ASPECTS OF THE READING PROCESS

DIMENSIONS OF THE READING ACT

IN CONSIDERING THE role of motor learning in relation to children learning to read it is essential to consider what reading is, what its dimensions are, and then to examine motor components of the reading process. Any attempt to describe or to define the reading process is an awesome task if the attempt is a serious one. (Yet such an assignment might well serve to humble, or even silence, the most verbal of critics of our schools' reading programs.) Such a task quickly reveals the complex nature of the reading process with its concomitant difficulties in identifying specific factors affecting success or lack of success in the reading act for each individual child.

The need to define or explain the reading process, however, is essential. It is well recognized that instructional procedures in reading are based on the teacher's concept of what reading is and how children learn to read. As stated in the Sixty-seventh Yearbook, Part II, Clymer states:

A clear concept of reading is not just an "academic" concern. A teacher's definition of reading influences every action he takes in the classroom.[1]

Clymer goes on to indicate the difficulty in formulating a definition of reading because of the many-faceted aspects of the process. "The areas of perception, psychology of learning, linguis-

[1] Clymer, Theodore: What is "reading"? Some current concepts. Innovation and change in reading instruction. *Sixty-seventh Yearbook of the National Society for the Study of Education, Part II*. Chicago. The University of Chicago Press, 1968, p. 8.

tics, social psychology, and language learning are a few of the fields contributing to an understanding of the reading process and the reading program."[2] This chapter will therefore attempt to define reading so that specific aspects of the process can be identified that will show how motor learning relates to and undergirds the reading act.

Current defining of the reading process invariably is presented within the context of the "total personality" of the reader. The multidimensional aspects of the reading process reflect the physical, the intellectual, the emotional, the social and environmental factors operating in the reading act.

While earlier decades found the nature of the reading act to be a more mechanistic process, such views gradually evolved to "getting meaning from the printed page," and finally to a more global comprehension process. In the Forty-eighth Yearbook, Part II, Gates defined the process:

> Reading is not a simple, mechanical skill; nor is it a narrow scholastic tool. Properly cultivated, it is essentially a thoughtful process. However, to say that reading is a "thought-getting" process is to give it too restricted a description. It should be developed as a complex organization of patterns of higher mental processes.[3]

Gates proceeded to state that reading embraces all types of thinking and imagining skills, that the reader "does more than understand and contemplate; his emotions are stirred; his attitudes and purposes modified; indeed, his innermost being is involved."[4]

Other definitions of reading also reflect increasing emphasis on the contemplative nature of processing information received from decoded visual symbols by thinking, analyzing, evaluating, projecting, and problem-solving.

DeBoer and Dallman in referring to reading as symbolic behavior through the association of visual symbols to auditory sym-

---

[2] *Ibid.* p. 8.

[3] Gates, Arthur I.: Character and purposes of the yearbook. reading in the elementary school. *Forty-eighth Yearbook of the National Society for the Study of Education, Part II.* Chicago. The University of Chicago Press, 1949, p. 3.

[4] *Ibid.* p. 4.

bols of language that in themselves serve as symbols of meaning, state:

> the process of reading involves a hierarchy of skills ranging from auditory and visual discrimination to such higher-order mental activities as organizing ideas, making generalizations, and drawing inferences.[5]

Spache and Spache define the reading process as (1) skill development according to Gray's description of reading (word recognition, literal understanding, critical evaluation and reaction, integration of concepts); (2) a visual act (involving acuity, coordination of the eyes, movement patterns, and eye span); (3) a perceptual act (a sequence involving the stimulus of the printed word, the processes of recognizing the word and attributing meaning to it based on the reader's previous experiences); (4) a reflection of cultural background (involving social factors of education, cultural interests, income level, family stability, vocational adjustments; and (5) a thinking process (involving cognition, memory, convergent and divergent reasoning, and evaluation). They conclude by adding that there are additional facets of the reading process, of its continuing relationship to the child's social and personal development and its resemblance to the learning process.[6]

Stauffer's summation of the myriad aspects of reading as a thinking process states:

> It would follow, then, that reading is a mental process requiring accurate word recognition, ability to call to mind particular meanings, and ability to shift or reassociate meanings—until the constructs or concepts presented are clearly grasped, critically evaluated, accepted and applied, or rejected. This means that knowledge gained through reading can increase understanding, and in turn, influence social and personal adjustment, enrich experience, and stimulate thinking."[7]

[5] DeBoer, John J., and Dallman, Martha: *The Teaching of Reading*, 3rd. ed. New York, Holt, Rinehart and Winston, Inc., 1970, p. 13.

[6] Spache, George D., and Spache, Evelyn B.: *Reading in the Elementary School*, 2nd ed. Boston, Allyn and Bacon, Inc., 1969, pp. 4–37.

[7] Stauffer, Russell G.: *Directing Reading Maturity as a Cognitive Process*. New York, Harper and Row, Publisher, 1969, p. 16.

Masland and Cratty have provided a more physically and motor-oriented definition of reading:

> Reading is a complex process involving the interaction and integration of ocular, perceptual, associative and motor abilities.
>
> In the process of reading, the individual must first regulate the larger muscles in his body to stabilize his visual apparatus, then he must scan the printed page through proper eye control. As he looks at the page, ocular processes must permit the forms on the page to be accurately transmitted to his retina and to his brain. He must differentiate the various simple and complex letter-word shapes.
>
> He must then relate these letter-word symbols to the verbal symbols and to the concepts for which they stand.—This process also presupposes an already existing verbal language structure bearing reasonable similarity to that of the written material."[8]

Within the last decade efforts to structure the components of the reading process have been directed to developing models, primarily to facilitate needed research in reading. Much attention has been given to Holmes' theoretical model, the Substrata-Factor Theory. In this hierarchial structure of subskills and their interaction in the reading process it is theorized that different centers of the brain store information received in visual, auditory, and kinesthetic (motor) forms, that the product of these interactions serve to process the stored information and produce power in reading. According to Holmes, "Within the limits of the genetic endowment of the brain of each individual, environmental experiences (internal as well as external) determine what bits of information will be encoded and how they will be organized."[9]

Clymer cites other models that have been utilized in recent efforts to structure the reading process, those of Guilford, McCullough, Kingston, Cleland, and Barrett. These models are comprehension oriented. Smith and Carrigan have developed one

---

[8] Masland, Richard L., and Cratty, Bryant J.: The nature of the reading process, The rationale of non-educational remedial methods. Calkins, Eloise O. (Ed.): *Reading Forum*, NIMDS Monograph No. 11. National Institute of Health.

[9] Holmes, Jack A.: Substrata-factor theory basic assumptions. *Reading Research Quarterly*, 1:3–28, Fall, 1965.

based on neurological considerations. The Gray and Robinson model, a revision of Gray's original, does focus on the broader dimension of reading that includes word perception as well as comprehension.[10]

In *Theoretical Models and Processes of Reading* further attempts have been made to review current theories and models of the mental structure and processes involved in the reading act. In speaking of the need for structuring our present knowledge and theorizing into models, the editors state:

> The more we understand the process [reading], the more likely we are to develop and devise instructional programs and materials that will enhance the reading abilities of our students, the ultimate goal of research in reading.[11]

Singer later categorizes models that have been developed since 1960 as being explicitly and implicitly formulated which can be further subgrouped as a logical organization of skills and abilities or processes for teaching purposes; process models based on psycholinguistic theory or neurological theory; a part of the reading process as perceptual, cognitive, an interaction between physiological and cognitive processes or comprehensive models of the reading act.[12]

One of the problems in defining reading or developing a reading model is differentiating clearly among processes required to read, the skills and abilities used in reading, and the procedures used to teach reading. According to Robinson all three are essential, but it is necessary to distinguish among them when developing a model of what reading is.[13]

According to Clymer, Strang's model meets Robinson's concerns and concludes, "While Strang gives only a partial analysis

[10] Clymer, *op. cit.* pp. 13–27.

[11] Singer, Harry, and Ruddell, Robert (Eds.): *Preface Theoretical Models and Processes of Reading.* Newark, Delaware, International Reading Association. p. xiii.

[12] *Ibid.* Theoretical Models of Reading: Implications for Teaching and Research. p. 148.

[13] Robinson, Helen M.: The major aspects of reading. Reading: seventy-five years of progress. H. Alan Robinson. (Ed.): *Supplementary Educational Monographs*, No. 96. Chicago, University of Chicago Press, 1966, pp. 22–32.

of each of these four aspects of a reading model, her four-part division is helpful in organizing our thinking about reading."[14] The divisions of Strang's model includes: "(a) products (the skills and abilities used in reading); (b) prerequisites (the traits and experiences necessary for successful reading); (c) the reading process (the chemistry, physiology, and psychology of the reading process); and (d) procedures (the techniques and conditions of instruction)."[15]

In speaking of Strang's model, Singer concludes that it also depicts the interrelationship of these divisions in the sequential scheme. This scheme is shown in Figure 2.

In this model Singer considers that the individual student (O) consists of a psychological model of the products, prerequisites, and processes within the reader. All the interacting systems and subsystems within the individual (physical, psychological, mental, attitudinal, knowledge, self-concept, desire to read) that function between stimulus input and response output are accommodated in this model. Procedures of instruction, classroom decor, the learning atmosphere and types of reading materials relate to the classroom situation (S). The resultant interaction involves the student's response (R) and leaves a trace (T) which is

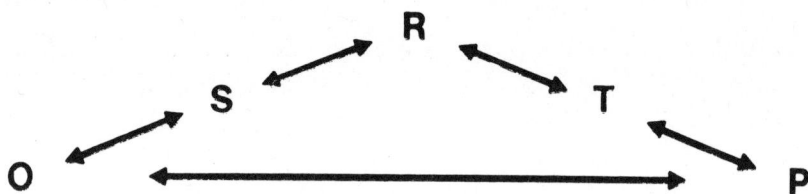

Figure 2. Strang's Model of Reading Process

Figure 2. The diagram indicates the relationships among the individual (O), the classroom reading situation (S), the individual's responses to the situation (R), the resulting memory traces (T), and the individual's perception (P) of the next situation. (Reprinted from "The Reading Process and Its Ramifications," In *Invitational Addresses, 1965.* Newark, Delaware: International Reading Association, 1965, pp. 49–74.)

[14] Clymer, *op. cit.* p. 14.
[15] *Ibid.,* p. 14.

stored within the individual's nervous system. This trace consequently influences the student's perception (P) of the next situation.[16]

Here is an example that clearly demonstrates that the process of reading, the skills used, the experiences necessary, are bound by the physical, intellectual, emotional and social environment of each reader, and that instructional procedures add to each of these dimensions.

MOTOR COMPONENTS OF READING

Now that the multidimensional aspects of the reading process have been identified it is essential to examine the motor components of the reading process. There are a number of motor components in the reading process. Two of these will be discussed in the present volume, the eye movements of the visual process itself and the sensori-motor aspects of perception and cognition. The motor components of subvocalization during the reading act will not be dealt with because it has little relevance to facilitating the learning-to-read process through motor learning.

Eye Movements in Reading

Early studies in reading focused on the visual act of reading as a means of better understanding of the process. Extensive research in this area continued through the 1940's. Such research resulted in the development of reading-eye cameras such as the Ophthalmograph (American Optical Company) by which eye movements could be recorded and analyzed.

From these studies the pattern of eye movements in the reading act is one of the eyes moving from left to right across the line of print with a return sweep to the next line, proceeding in a left-to-right direction again. This rhythmic movement line after line is broken by fixations as the eyes move across the line and regressions or backward movements.

At fixation points the eyes are not in motion. It is at this

[16] Singer *op. cit.* p. 174.

moment, however, that the vision is not blurred by movement and the visual act of reading takes place. The time of a "fixation" may vary from a third to a fourth of a second and is affected by the skill development of the reader and the difficulty of the material. Ninety per cent of the time spent in reading is accounted for by fixation points when the reader is going through the "seeing," the word recognition, and the association process.

Regressions occur when there is a breakdown in the word recognition and association aspects of the reading process. The reader may regress along the same line or several lines in order to arrive at word recognition or comprehension of the idea being presented. Spache and Spache caution that "An excessive proportion of unknown words, inadequate experiences with the multiple meanings of words, and reading matter which is much too complex for the child's experiences all promote a faulty reading pattern and lack of progress in reading."[17]

Eye span is another term utilized in describing the visual act. Eye span is the span of recognition during the moment of "fixation." For the elementary-grade child the eye span is limited to the point that there is an average of two fixation points per word. The limitations of the eye span also indicates the demand upon the eyes in terms of the number of times the eyes converge in perfect alignment to focus at each "fixation."

As a visual task, adequate vision for reading calls for coordination and motility with accurate binocular shifts from point to point, accurate focus and accommodation to distance, a fine degree of parallel or coordinated action of both eyes and left-to-right directional attack.

Difficulties of function in eye movements result in loss of place, omissions, excessive repetitions, and slow rate. Defects in coordination, motility, directional attack, and form perception prevent development of desirable pattern of eye movement.[18]

When there is evidence of deficiencies in visual perception or eye-hand coordination these authors recommend developmental training should be given. They proceed to outline three major

[17] Spache and Spache, op. cit. p. 9.
[18] Ibid. pp. 11–12.

types of visual training for perception and discrimination. These include (1) directionality, or orientation to direction; (2) ocular motility, or promoting coordinated movements of both eyes; and (3) form perception, or discrimination of similarities and differences in designs, figures, and word-like forms. The authors have included a number of sequential and varied types of activities related to each of these areas for training in visual perception. They are described in detail and can serve as a specific help to the classroom teacher, particularly of primary-grade children. They have also listed a number of materials that are available for developing these skills.[19]

The Sensori-Motor Aspects of Perception and Cognition in Reading

Perception in the reading act is a functional sequence involving the stimulus of the printed words, the process of recognizing the word, and assigning meaning to it based on the reader's previous past experiences. At this point reading must also be considered a symbolic function in that it allows the reader to cognize through representational thought. Stauffer sees the development of the symbol system language as the foundation of cognitive development:

> The development of a symbol system, particularly language, increases the power for organizing acts of information processes into more integrated and long-range problem-solving efforts. It also increases the child's ability to transcend immediate experience and transforms the regularities of experience with greater power and flexibility. So we see that, as the child's symbol system develops from action to image to word, it becomes an increasingly important means of knowing. This is why so much of the research is focused on the transition from action or enactive representation to images or iconic representation and to language or symbolic representation.[20]

It is at this point that the present authors feel that reading instruction oftentimes becomes inconsistent with what is declared essential in the reading process or what is recommended for the

[19] *Ibid.* pp. 197–217.
[20] Stauffer, *op. cit.* p. 341.

learning-to-read environment of children. With the ever-increasing emphasis on the higher-level cognitive processing in the reading experience there seems to be an inordinate focus on words in the abstract context rather than in the reality context.

In discussing the vagueness and faultiness of understanding in the verbalism of children, Harris and Sipay state, "An unfortunately large share of school learning in the past has been the memorization of verbal statements that are misunderstood or only partially understood because they have no real connection with the child's experience."[21] They comment further, "Many of the important concepts of science and the social studies are difficult for children to understand because they are highly abstract and have been learned with insufficient reference to experience."[22] Their statement, "Direct experience is the primary basis for concepts and ideas. Verbal explanation is secondary; it helps to clarify experience but cannot completely replace it,"[23] is certainly an apt one.

Language growth is described within the total context of child development. As the child moves to the readiness stage for reading, his physical growth and environment are described as characteristically physically-oriented. During the first years in school the child uses physically-oriented activities not as an end in themselves but as a means of manipulating the environment for other purposes. Such activities gradually include those involving finer muscle coordinations. During this period there is also the characteristically tremendous physical energy which manifests itself in physical activity as mentioned in relation to the basal metabolism rate in Chapter Two. Russell relates these characteristics of children's physical and mental growth to the organization of the reading program:

[21] Harris, Albert J., and Sipay, Edward R.: *Effective Teaching of Reading,* 2nd ed. New York, David McKay Company, 1971, p. 269.

[22] *Ibid.,* p. 269.

[23] *Ibid.,* p. 267.

[*] The concerns of Harris and Sipay relate directly to the underlying principle of the book: Humphrey, James H., and Sullivan, Dorothy D.: *Teaching Slow Learners Through Active Games.* Springfield, Illinois, Charles C Thomas Publisher, 1970.

The application of this physical development to the primary reading program are rather direct. Children in the first grade should engage in many physical activities and thus need a program involving something more than just sitting.[24]

It is interesting to note that his concept of the use of physically-oriented activities was limited to pacing and spacing with reading-oriented activities rather than using motor-learning as a means of developing reading skills.[25]

Russell further states that primary-age children are essentially interested in the here and now, that while their horizons begin to broaden for these children, experiences must be real and related to past experiences if they are to become part of the child's living. The reading program in method and content must grow out of the child's immediate environment and experiences, developing fairly concrete ideas rather than abstract generalizations with an emphasis on group membership and participation.[26]

Walcott stresses that language develops as a counterpart to exploratory action. It serves as a record of experience as well as comprehension of things discovered and their relationship to other things.[27]

In discussing meaningfulness and the transfer of learning Kuethe brings out that students can rapidly assimilate new material if it is meaningful in terms of what has been learned previously. "Actually, meaningfulness is always dependent upon past learning to some extent: indeed the term implies a relationship to the past."[28] He goes on to warn the teacher not to be subtle in helping students make these connections. He considers it a common error to assume the relationship is obvious to students because it is so obvious to the teacher.[29]

[24] Russell, David H.: *Children Learn to Read.* New York, Ginn and Company 1961, p. 81.

[25] *Ibid.,* p. 81.

[26] *Ibid.,* pp. 81–83.

[27] Walcott, Fred G.: Language and its functions in life. Herrick, Virgil E. and Jacobs, Leland B. (Eds.): *Children and the Language Arts.* Englewood Cliffs, New Jersey, Prentice-Hall, 1955, p. 41.

[28] Kuethe, James L.: *The Teaching-Learning Process. Keystones of Education Series.* Chicago, Illinois, Scott, Foresman and Company, 1968. p. 77.

[29] *Ibid.* p. 77.

Stauffer, in his summary of cognitive development and its relationship to reading instruction states, "Children must be active and required to act on material things as well as hypothetical ideas, and they should do this in social collaboration or in a group effort."[30]

Recognition has been given to the need for training in visual perception skills. The sensori-motor aspects of the real experience, the bringing of physical reality to the printed word and page through proprioception, are cited over and over again as facilitating and enhancing perception and cognition. The naturalness of the physically-oriented activity for beginning and early readers is recognized.

The authors recognize that the reading act ultimately emphasizes the representational nature of word symbols, that the higher levels of cognition are abstract. But it is not an either-or situation. There is general agreement that the physical reality of concrete experiences aids comprehension. There is evidence that there is need for increased emphasis upon the use of the physical reality of the child in his learning-to-read efforts. Later chapters will outline several activities utilizing motor learning that have been developed and found effective in skills development and establishing interest in and positive attitudes toward reading.

[30] Stauffer, *op. cit.* p. 351.

CHAPTER FOUR

PERCEPTUAL-MOTOR DEVELOPMENT AND READING

IT WAS INDICATED in Chapter One that the branch of motor learning involving perceptual-motor development is concerned with the correction, or at least some degree of improvement, of certain motor deficiencies, especially those associated with fine coordinations. Proponents of this type of training see a need for it with certain neurologically handicapped children who have various types of learning disabilities, that is, identifiable conditions that prevent the adequate accumulation, retention, and utilization of knowledge.

It has been suggested that the child with disorganization in perceptual areas, stemming from an impairment of the central nervous system, may be affected in any of three ways:[1] He may be unable to learn to read, to conceptualize or reason, or to convert visual impressions into meaningful information. None of these perceptual difficulties is likely to be noticed until the child has been in school long enough for it to show up as a handicap. Diagnosis of the specific types of perceptual difficulty is extremely important as a basis for planning an effective educational program for the child.

Ordinarily, attempts are made to correct or improve fine motor control problems through a sequence of motor competencies, which tend to follow a definite hierarchy of development. Methods of accomplishing this, range from highly structured extremely vigorous physical exercise programs, to unstructured more creative types of programs.

[1] Kappelman, Murray M., and Ganter, Robert L.: A clinic for children with learning disabilities. *Children, 17,* 4, July-August, 1970.

As we proceed with our discussions in this chapter we need to do so with a certain degree of caution. While a great deal of attention is currently being focused upon perceptual-motor programs, it should be made luminously clear that such programs are not a panacea for all of the learning problems of children. However, if these types of programs (1) are geared to meet the individual needs of children; (2) remain within the realm of valid educational objectives; and (3) take into account the development of the child's *total* personality, they can become an important part of a multidisciplinary approach to some of the learning problems of children.

We should point out that in attempts to make diagnoses of specific difficulties we need to take into account that not all learning difficulties stem from the problems previously suggested. For example, many children suffer emotional problems which encumber their learning ability. Others are lacking in motivation which is often caused by the stilted and sterile conditions in the school itself. The learning of some is influenced by uneven and/or immature development, and of course there are those who simply do not possess sufficient intellectual capacity to learn.

In the subsequent discussions of perceptual-motor development, the reader should take certain important factors into account. As mentioned previously, there is much current interest in the use of perceptual-motor developmental methods with elementary-school-age children. It is most important that the reader consider that the many research studies conducted in the area of perceptual-motor development do *not* present clear-cut and definitive evidence to support the notion that such programs result in academic achievement. There are too many other variables that can contribute to academic gains made by children. Such factors as normal maturation, the influence of testing, systematic training in the focus of attention that perceptual-motor training involves, along with the ever important aspect of teaching ability, certainly need to be considered. Nevertheless, although the findings in support of perceptual-motor training are much more exploratory than definitive, this type of training should have a place in the school curriculum provided there is sufficient supervision and well-qualified personnel. Perceptual-motor training *should not be used in place of* validated teaching procedures, but rather in addition to the regular school curriculum in specific cases where it is warranted.

MEANING OF TERMS

The term "perception" is concerned with how we obtain information from the environment through the various sensory modalities and what we make of it. As far as the reading process is concerned, it particularly refers to the *visual perception* of graphic symbols. In the present context the term "motor" is concerned with the impulse for motion resulting in a change of position through various forms of body movement. Espenschade[2] suggests that when the two terms are put together (perceptual-motor) the implication is an organization of interpretation of sensory data, with related voluntary motor responses.

PERCEPTUAL-MOTOR SKILLS

There is a considerable amount of agreement among child development specialists that there is no simple distinction between a perceptual skill and a motor skill. This has no doubt led to the development of the term "perceptual-motor skills." In fact, to some extent this term seems to be supplanting such terms as "neuro-muscular" and "sensory-motor."

In general, the current postulation appears to be that if perceptual training improves perceptual and motor abilities, then because of the fact that perceptual and motor abilities are so highly interrelated and interdependent each upon the other, it should follow that training in perception should facilitate perceptual-motor problems. There is abundant objective support of the notion that training of perception can improve per-

---

[2] Espenschade, Anna S.: Perceptual-motor development in children. *The Academy Papers*, No. 1, The American Academy of Physical Education, 1968, pp: 14–20.

ceptual ability. Although there is not a great deal of clear-cut evidence to support the idea that perceptual-motor training does increase the performance ability in perceptual-motor skills, some research, such as the work of Johnson and Fretz[3] has indicated that certain kinds of perceptual-motor skills can be significantly improved for certain children who take part over a specified period of time in a children's physical developmental program.

What then are the perceptual-motor skills? Generally, the kinds of skills that fit into a combination of manual coordinations and eye-hand skills may be considered a valid classification.

Visual perception is based on sensorimotor experiences that depend on visual acuity, eye-hand coordination, left-right body orientation, and other visual-spatial abilities including visual sequencing.[4]

Studies have shown a positive correlation between difficulties in visual perception and achievement in reading. Strang cites numerous studies in concluding that, "In general, average and superior readers tend to perform better than retarded readers on tests of perceptual differentiation, tests of closure, and measures of lag in perceptual-motor maturation."[5]

Indication of a child's eye-hand coordination may be observed as he bounces or throws a ball, erases a chalkboard, drives a nail, cuts paper with scissors, copies a design, ties his shoe laces, picks up a small object from the floor, or replaces a cap on a pen. Strang states that "In reading, the child shows difficulty in eye-hand coordination by his inability to keep his place in reading, to find the place again in the pattern of printed words, and to maintain the motor adjustment as long as is necessary to comprehend word, phrase, or sentence. His tendency to skip lines may arise from inability to direct the eyes accurately to the beginning of the next line."[6]

[3] Johnson, Warren R., and Fretz, Bruce R.: Changes in perceptual-motor skills after a children's physical development program. *Perceptual and Motor Skills*, April, 1967.

[4] Strang, Ruth: *Diagnostic Teaching of Reading*, 2nd ed. New York, McGraw-Hill Book Company, 1969, p. 153.

[5] *Ibid.*

[6] *Ibid.*, p. 181.

Depending upon a variety of extenuating circumstances, perceptual-motor skills require various degrees of voluntary action. The basic striking and catching skills are examples of this type and are important in certain kinds of active game activities. That is, receiving an object (catching) such as a ball, and hitting (striking) an object, ordinarily with an implement, such as batting a ball. Other kinds of skills in this category, but not related to game activities, include sorting of objects, finger painting, and bead stringing. There is another group of tasks perceptual-motor in nature which involve such factors as choice, discrimination, and problem solving. These may be found in various types of intelligence tests and the ability to perform the tasks under certain kinds of conditions are utilized.

There are certain tasks that are perceptual-motor in character that are done with one hand. At a high level of performance this could involve receiving a ball with one hand in a highly organized sports activity. At a very low level, in reaching for or grasping an object a baby will do so with one hand.

In some kinds of *visual* tasks requiring the use of one eye, there appears to be an eye preference. In reading, it is believed that one eye may lead or be dominant. In tasks where one eye is used and one hand is used, most people will use those on the same side of the body. This is to say that there is *lateral dominance*. In the case of those who use the left eye and right hand or the opposite of this, *mixed dominance* is said to exist. Some studies suggest that mixed dominance may have a negative effect on motor coordination, but perhaps just as many investigators report that this is not the case.

Masland and Cratty have summarized the research on the relationship between handedness, brain dominance and reading disability and characterize the research as "voluminous, often contradictory, and most confusing."[7] The following conclusions are based on their broad review of the research.

---

[7] Masland, Richard L., and Cratty, Bryant J.: The nature of the reading process, the rational non-educational remedial methods, Calkins, Eloise O. (Ed.): *Reading Forum,* NIMDS Monograph No. 11, Department of Health, Education and Welfare, Washington, D.C.

1. It has not been demonstrated that laterality of hand or eye dominance, or mixed dominance bear a direct relationship to poor reading.
2. There is a very low correlation between handedness or eyedness and brain dominance for language. There is no evidence that changing handedness will influence the lateralization of other functions.
3. There are neither theoretical nor empirical data to support efforts to change handedness or eyedness as a means of improving reading ability.

A condition often related to dominance as far as reading is concerned is that of *reversals*. One type of reversal (static) refers to a child seeing letters reversed such as *n* and *b* appearing as *u* and *d*. In another type (kinetic) the child may see the word "no" as "on." In some instances it has been found that children with the kinetic type of reversal also have a condition known as "arhythmia" (lack of rhythm). Attempts have been made to provide certain kinds of rhythmic movements for such children in order to correct this condition. It is possible that this approach may have much to commend it and varying degrees of success have been attained with it. More generally, procedures involving kinesthetic techniques of tracing words has been utilized.

At one time reversals were considered as possibly related to dominance. However, later studies negated this earlier view. In more recent years studies tend to support the contention that problems of visual perception, spatial orientation, and recognition of form rather than dominance patterns result in children making reversals.

Perhaps some mention should be made regarding the most satisfactory ways of presenting perceptual-motor skills to children. Although a great deal of evidence has not been accumulated to support one method over another the work of Smith is of interest.[8]

The purpose of this study was to determine the extent to which kindergarten children were ready for first grade experi-

[8] Smith, Paul: Perceptual-motor skills and readiness of kindergarten children, *Journal of Health, Physical Education and Recreation*, April 1970, pp. 43–44.

ences and to attempt to compare the effects of three methods of presenting perceptual-motor skills on the reading readiness of randomly placed kindergarten children. The results indicated that there was no significant differences between the directed and problem solving methods of teaching these skills. However, there was a greater mean score gain in the combined directed *and* problem solving groups when compared with a group where color-coded targets were used rather than verbalized directions for the movements. Thus, it was generalized that just doing the movements will not bridge all perceptual-motor learning gaps. It appeared that there is a greater understanding and transfer of learning if the direction of each movement is used to reinforce the movement.

PERCEPTUAL-MOTOR PROGRAMS

In general, organized programs that involve perceptual-motor training fall into the two broad categories of those that are considered to be *structured* and those that are considered to be *unstructured.* Since there are various degrees of structuring of activities that make up a given program, a considerable amount of overlapping can exist from one program to another. For example, there could be some degree of structuring in a program that for all practical purposes would be classified as unstructured.

The structured program of perceptual-motor training is based on the notion that some form of structured physical activity can contribute to the development of a higher learning capacity for children with certain kinds of learning disabilities.[9] The unstructured type of program tends to be more creative in nature and is not dependent upon a set of more or less "fixed" exercises.

Play therapists have been aware of the value of the unstructured type of approach for years as shown by the following summary of a study reported by Bills some years ago.[10]

[9] Footlik, S. Willard: Perceptual-motor training and cognitive achievement: A survey of the literature. *Journal of Learning Disabilities*, Vol. 3, No. 1, January 1970, p. 42.

[10] Bills, Robert E.: Nondirective play therapy with retarded readers. *Journal of Consulting Psychology*, Vol. 14, 1950, pp. 140–149.

This study was an investigation of the effects of individual and group play on the reading level of retarded readers. As a result of the play therapy experiences it was concluded that (1) significant changes in reading ability occurred as a result of the play therapy experiences; and (2) personal changes may occur in nondirective play therapy in as little as six individual and three group play therapy sessions.

It should be clearly understood that it is *not* the purpose here to either extol or condemn any of the various approaches to perceptual-motor training in the form of organized programs. On the contrary, we simply wish to identify some representative examples of perceptual-motor programs that fall within the range of structuring and unstructuring previously mentioned.

1. *Glenhaven Achievement Center*

This Center is under the direction of Dr. Newell C. Kephart, one of the early exponents of perceptual-motor training for children with learning disabilities. It is located at Colorado State University, P.O. Box 2153, Fort Collins, Colorado.

This program is based on the principle that the accumulation of motor information is basic to all other perceptual-motor skills. And further, that with slow learning children it is often necessary to return to basic motor patterns to allow the child to recapitulate the process of development by which finer and more complex patterns are achieved.

2. *Marianne Frostig Center of Educational Therapy*

This Center is under the direction of Dr. Marianne Frostig and is located at 5981 Venice Boulevard, Los Angeles, California. This program devotes its services to children with learning disabilities. According to its founder, "the physical education programs at the Center are based on research and designed to systematically train children, so that they will no longer find their bodies to be strange obstructive adjuncts, but responsive tools with which to joyfully master the environment."[11]

---

[11] Frostig, Marianne: Training the child's basic abilities through physical education. *Center Newsletter*, June, 1968.

3. *Program of the Reading Research Foundation*

This program is under the direction of S. Willard Footlik and its main office is located at 814 Diversey Parkway, Chicago, Illinois. One of the stated major goals of this Foundation is to make perceptual-motor training available to as many children as possible who are not achieving their full potential.

4. *University of Maryland Children's Physical Developmental Clinic*

This Clinic was organized by its present Director, Dr. Warren R. Johnson, Professor of Physical Education and Health at the University of Maryland. It is located in the Health Education Department, University of Maryland, College Park, Maryland.

The basic purpose of the Clinic is to improve certain aspects of the "total fitness for living" of children who are referred to it. The approach is primarily in terms of physical activity, through which the child may (1) gain greater awareness of confidence in his body and what he can do with it; (2) acquire and/or improve basic skills which not only increase the range of his movement capabilities and satisfactions, but also heighten his ability to functon effectively in the activities of other children and thus provide a basis for the acquisition of greater social skill; and (3) increase the basic efficiency, stamina and power of his body-machine.

All of the programs identified here, as well as numerous others, have their enthusiastic supporters. These programs utilize a variety of approaches in attempting to solve learning problems of children. Regardless of the approach used and the degree of structuring in executing the approach, any program should take into account the total personality development concept. It is important to indicate that most perceptual-motor programs have as their objective improvement of self concept and ability to control the physical environment, rather than direct growth in reading.

PERCEPTUAL-MOTOR MEDIA

When thought of as an educational term, "media" has been defined by one authoritative source as "Printed and audiovisual forms of communication and their accompanying technology."[12] As far as perceptual-motor media are concerned, the meaning of media needs to be extended to include the various types of instruments, machines, and apparatus used to promote perceptual-motor development, in addition to all forms of auditory and/or visual input.

It will *not* be the purpose of this section of the Chapter to go into depth with regard to *all* possible perceptual-motor media, or necessarily with regard to all of the most recent innovations. This is to say that in no sense should the material presented here be considered to be theoretically complete. On the contrary, it will be the major function here simply to familiarize the reader with some representative examples of perceptual-motor media. In some instances suggestions will be made with regard to the purpose of the media and how they might be applied. For our purposes here we will arbitrarily classify the media as either *standard* or *specialized*. "Standard" means those kinds of media that are used in various other situations not specifically concerned with perceptual-motor training. "Specialized" means those kinds of media that have been pretty much designed especially for use in perceptual-motor training.

Standard

Aquatic Activities

Aquatic experiences can begin by age two. The water is a perfect medium for allowing children to experience the tactile sense over the total body surface, the delicious freedom from gravitational force, the sensing of pressure on hands, arms, legs, and feet that tell one he is making himself move, and the use of the temperature receptors of the skin that signal whether a leg or an

[12] American Library Association, Standards for School media programs, 50 Huron Street, Chicago, Illinois, 1969, p. xv.

arm is in or out of the water.[13] The importance of these kinds of experiences in perceptual-motor training are reflected in the program of developmental movement education for children ages two to five sponsored by the Department of Physical Education for Women at Purdue University. The Coordinator of this program, Dr. Marguerite Clifton, gives the following objectives of the aquatics area of the program.[14]

1. To foster the achievement of ease and self-confidence in the water through individually planned experiences tailored to each child's departure point and progress through the program.
2. To improve performance, as directed toward four areas:
   (a) adjustment, buoyancy and balance skills
   (b) propulsion skills
   (c) face in water and breathing skills
   (d) entry skills

Dr. Clifton explains the program as follows:[15]

Similar age children are in the pool together, each with his own instructor in a one to one ratio. The length of time in the water ranges from 20 minutes for two-year-olds to 40 minutes for five-year-olds. Prior experience beyond 'bathtub splashing' varies considerably. Over half of the children, however, usually have not had experience in some body of water, be it pool, lake, or ocean.

Flotation devices of any kind are seldom used. Thus, the environment requires the child to rely on the use of his own body in order to stay afloat. One of the real difficulties sometimes encountered is occasioned by the children whose parents have used flotation supports on the child when at the lake or beach. Generally, this child takes a longer time to orient himself to the pool experience.

A sequential list of potential experiences arranged within the

[13] Smith, Hope M.: Implications for movement education experiences drawn from perceptual-motor research. *Journal of Health, Physical Education and Recreation,* April 1970, p. 33.

[14] Clifton, Marguerite: A developmental approach to perpetual-motor experiences. *Journal of Health, Physical Education and Recreation,* April, 1970, p. 35.

[15] *Ibid.*

aquatic objectives cited above provides teachers with an array of choices for use with each youngster depending on his individual progress and occasional remissions. Availability of a poolside record-keeping system enables teachers to record specific behavior information at the conclusion of one time block and review the progress record of the next child before he enters the pool area.

The pool balcony is a favorite spot for parents to observe. The child's need for constant reinforcement is evidenced by frequent searching for mother's face at the beginning of the program. Gradually with the child's increasing skillfulness he becomes less dependent on reinforcement from parents.

The depth of the water, even in the shallow area of the pool, precludes the children's being able to stand on the bottom of the pool with their heads above water. Each child soon adjusts to his teacher, however, and gains complete trust in the supportive functions of his instructor.

The program's emphasis on achieving individual comfort and self-confidence through mastery of skills was not fully understood by some swimming-stroke-oriented parents. It should be noted, too, that parental pressure and expectations for achievement are observed far more frequently in the aquatic area than in the other two areas (gymnasium area and perceptual-motor area). This undoubtedly is due to the parents' superior knowledge of swimming per se and the ease with which one observes gains or remissions in performance in this situation.

Games

According to some authorities disturbance in body image or lack of body awareness, and not lack of movement skills is a possible cause of some disturbances of visual perception.[16] Thus, it could be assumed that improvement of body image could have a positive effect on visual perceptual ability of children. An example of a game that can contribute to the development of body awareness is one called *Busy Bee*. In this game the chil-

[16] Ayres, A. Jean: Summary of presentation to Los Angeles County Elementary Guidance Association: Types of perceptual-motor deficits in children with learning difficulties, April, 1964.

dren are in pairs facing each other and dispersed around the activity area. One child who is the *caller* is in the center of the area. He makes calls such as "shoulder to shoulder," "toe to toe," or "hand to hand." (In the early stages of the game it might be well to have the teacher do the calling). As the calls are made, the paired children go through the appropriate motions with their partners. After a few calls, the caller will shout "Busy Bee!" This is the signal for every child to get a new partner, including the caller. The child who does not get a partner can become the new caller.

This game has been experimented with in the following manner: As the children played the game, the teacher made them aware of the location of various parts of the body in order to develop the concept of full body image.

Before the game was played, the children were asked to draw a picture of themselves. Many did not know how to begin, and others omitted some of the major limbs in their drawings. After playing Busy Bee, the children were again asked to draw a picture of themselves. This time they were more successful. All of the drawings had bodies, heads, arms, and legs. A few even had teeth and hair.[17]

Another example of how certain games can help children with learning difficulties is seen with children with slow reaction time. This is the amount of elapsed time that it takes a person to get an overt response started after receiving a stimulus or the stimulus to response interval. Such children ordinarily have difficulty in processing input from an auditory and/or visual stimulus. When this occurs some teachers tend to feel that the child is not interested and lacks enthusiasm. This condition can be improved over a period of time by games requiring auditory and/or visual input as a starting signal. One such game is *Crows and Cranes* which involves auditory input. The game is played in the following manner.

The playing area is divided by a center line. On opposite ends of the area are drawn lines parallel to the center line. The

[17] Humphrey, James H., and Sullivan, Dorothy D.: *Teaching Slow Learners Through Active Games.* Springfield, Illinois, Charles C Thomas, Publisher, 1970, p. 20.

group is divided into two teams. The children of one team are designated as Crows and take position on one side of the area, with the base line on their side serving as their safety zone. The members of the other team are designated as Cranes and take positions on the other side of the area, with their base line as a safety zone. The teacher stands to one side of the area by the center line. The teacher then calls out either, "Crows" or "Cranes." If the teacher calls the Crows, they turn and run to their base line to avoid being tagged. The Cranes attempt to tag their opponents before they cross their base line. The Cranes score a point for each Crow tagged. The Crows and Cranes then return to their places, and the teacher proceeds to call one of the groups; play continues in the same manner. As the teacher observes certain children reacting slowly they can be grouped together.

The game of *Black and White* is played in the same manner but uses visual input. One team is the Blacks and the other, the Whites. An object, black on one side and white on the other is tossed into the air. If it comes down on the black side, the Blacks run for their base line and vice versa.

Rhythmic Activities

The term "rhythm" is derived from the Greek word *rhythmos* which means "measured motion." One need only to look at the functions of the human body to see the importance of rhythm in the life of children. The heart beats in rhythm, the digestive processes function in rhythm, and breathing is done in rhythm.[18] It is a well-known fact that rhythm is present to at least some degree in all forms of voluntary human movement. For example, several decades ago H'Doubler[19] commented that . . . any movement, no matter how poorly coordinated or executed, has rhythm, but a rhythm that is different from that of the well-coordinated performance.

---

[18] Humphrey, James H.: *Child Learning Through Elementary School Physical Education.* Dubuque, Iowa, William C. Brown, Co., 1966, p. 74.
[19] H'Doubler, Margaret: An interpretation of rhythm. *Journal of Health and Physical Education,* September, 1932.

In reporting about neurological dysfunctioning in the visual-perceptual-auditory-sensory-motor areas, McClurg implied that disabled readers frequently lack coordination in such basic motor movements as walking and running. And further, that motor rhythm is often lacking in persons with reading, writing and spelling problems.[20]

The importance of rhythm in the reading problem of kinetic reversal was mentioned earlier in the chapter. It is interesting to note that in this general connection, Drake found that by working with dyslexic children in fine motor skills such as handwriting, and patterned motor skills—especially folk dancing—improvement in reading was in evidence.[21]

Without question it appears logical to assume that rhythmic activities can be a very important medium in perceptual-motor training. Perhaps for most children the most successful type to use would be creative rhythms, where the child responds by expressing himself in a way that the rhythmical accompaniment makes him feel. This approach will give the child free self-direction in space, as well as self-control in that he is not involved with a partner in a more formalized rhythmic activity. In this regard, it should be mentioned, however, that there is also merit in some cases in performing a rhythmic activity within the framework of an established pattern. This is particularly true as far as emotional release is concerned. Mental hygienists know that some persons can express themselves with more spontaneity in a relatively "structured" situation than in one where they have more freedom (possibly a factor in the work reported by Drake above). Such persons, when they skip, dance, clap and whirl to the rhythm of the music may be expressing themselves with an abandon that is not possible when they are free to express themselves in any way they wish.[22]

[20] McClurg, William H.: The neurophysiological basis of reading disabilities. *The Reading Teacher*, April, 1969.

[21] Drake, Charles: Reading 'riting, and rhythm. *The Reading Teacher*, December, 1964.

[22] Layman, Emma M.: *In Science and Medicine of Exercise and Sports*, 2nd ed. (Eds.): Johnson, W.R., and Buskirk, E.R. Harper and Row Publishers, New York 1973.

Stunt and Tumbling Activities

Stunts are concerned predominantly with certain kinds of imitations such as animal imitations and the performance of a variety of feats that utilize such factors as balance, coordination, flexibility, agility, and strength. Tumbling involves various kinds of body rolls and body springs that encourage the development of these same abilities. Stunt activities which involve imitations of animals are very interesting and appealing to young children. Since reading is a perceptual skill involving bilateral movement, animal imitations and other stunts involving such movement might be used to advantage. A very important factor here is that this type of activity has a sort of "built in" motivation which guarantees to an extent that the child will happily pursue the activity purely for the joy and pleasure he receives from it.

Tumbling activities which involve some of the simple rolls are very suitable for the young child. A factor here is that there is an opportunity to "put into play" those parts of the body, for example the torso, which is less sensitive to tactile perception, than other body parts. A specific example of such an activity is the "log roll." This tumbling activity is performed by having the child lie on his back with his arms and legs extended. He then proceeds to roll over and over, as a log, on a matted area.

Trampoline

The trampoline can be particularly useful in developing better awareness of self, and concepts of spatial relationships. Kephart, one of the early exponents of the value of the trampoline in perceptual-motor training comments as follows:[23]

Not only must the child learn a dynamic relationship to the center of gravity and maintain a dynamic balance, but he must maintain these coordinations under changing relationships. In addition, the changes in these relationships are not the result of his own effort directly, but are dependent in a large part on the trampoline and its functions. Thus, the timing and rhythm of

---

[23] Kephart, Newell C.: *The Slow Learner in the Classroom.* Columbus, Ohio, Charles E. Merrill Books, 1960.

his activity are dictated by the spring of his trampoline rather than directly determined by his own movements. In activities on the ground, the child can adjust his movements to the rhythm pattern of his muscles. Thus, if the neurological innervation to one or more muscle groups loses its rhythm, he merely adjusts his movements to this change. On the trampoline, such adjustment is not possible, since the rhythm is dictated by the device. Therefore, he must learn to maintain adequate and constant rhythms in his neuromuscular coordination which are demanded in few other activities. Thus, mere activity of bouncing on the trampoline contributes to body image and spatial relationships within the body.

Some research has been conducted in connection with the benefits to be derived from the use of the trampoline as a perceptual-motor medium. An example is the work of McCants.[24] In a controlled study to determine the effects of an eight-week instructional program of trampolining upon selected measures of the physical fitness of mentally retarded and emotionally disturbed children in a special school, he found that the experimental group improved significantly in all tests. It was also observed that there were other improvements in the experimental group in the way of classroom performance, social adjustment, morale and confidence. An interesting aside to this study was that the investigator was employed immediately to continue the program for the rest of the children in the school.

Some perceptual-motor specialists have developed a series of trampoline activities. One such progressive sequence has been developed and published by Lyle K. Trexler.[25] The sequence of activities is accompanied by directions for their use.

Balance Beam

Activities on the balance beam can help the child maintain his relationship to gravity and at the same time help to develop space awareness and directionally related movements. In con-

[24] McCants, Robert: *Effects of an Eight-week Trampoline Instruction Program on Certain Measures of the Physical Fitness of Retarded Children,* masters thesis. University of Maryland, College Park, Maryland, 1962.
[25] Trexler, Lyle K.: The Trampoline: A training device for children with perceptual-motor problems. *Academic Therapy,* Winter, 1969–70.

nection with the use of the balance beam, Smith makes the following important observation:[26]

Autokinetic movement, the visual illusion that gives one the impression that a stationary object is in motion, occurs during prolonged periods of constant visual focus on an object.

. . . when teaching activities requiring students to maintain continuous and prolonged focus on a stationary object or spot (such as balance beam exercises demand), the student should be encouraged to occasionally shift his visual focus by a few degrees right or left. It may be helpful to provide some focal point that is in constant slight motion. For beginners, a blinking light might be provided on standards at each end of the beam. Such a teaching aid may produce more efficient motor response in balance activities.

Attempts to study the relationship between reading and ability to perform dynamic balance have yielded varying results. In one such study Walker[27] compared balance beam walking test scores with reading readiness test scores of 162 first-grade children. On the basis of his data he generalized that: (1) there seemed to be a tendency for first-grade children scoring high or low in the reading readiness test to score respectively high or low on the balance beam walking test; (2) there seemed to be a much greater relationship between balance beam walking test scores and reading readiness test scores exhibited by girls than boys; and (3) girls tended to score higher than boys on the balance beam walking test. It is important to recognize that these are not cause and effect relationships but coexisting behaviors.

Ball Handling Activities

Activities with inflated balls include tapping (ordinarily referred to as bouncing), throwing to a partner or target, and catching. These skills can often be useful in helping children develop eye-hand coordination, timing, and bilaterality.

Ordinarily, children with eye-hand coordination problems

[26] Smith, Hope M., *op. cit.* p. 31.

[27] Walker, James: *A Comparison of Lee-Clark Reading Readiness Scores with a Test of Balance Using Selected First Grade Children*, masters thesis. University of Maryland, College Park, Maryland 1963.

have difficulty catching a ball, not necessarily because of a motor response, but perhaps more likely because of slowness in eye movement. It may be a good practice with some children, to simply roll a ball slowly across the surface area and have them follow it with their eyes. Several children can sit in a circle and roll the ball back and forth to each other. Later they can work on catching a ball at a short distance in the air. A beach ball or even a balloon may be good to begin with because the lighter weight of this type of object will cause it to move more slowly through the air. Under these conditions of being able to follow the object visually, the child should be more successful in catching it.

Tapping a ball can be used to advantage to improve timing. Sometimes it is helpful to accompany tapping with some sort of rhythm. Many children in their first experience with tapping tend to "slap" the ball hard, causing it to rebound in a way that is difficult to control. One way to help to avoid this is to suggest that the ball is a friend and should be treated as such ("as you might pat your puppydog").

Most of the balls used for the purposes indicated here are not inflated to pound pressure. On the other hand, specifications of some indicate inflating the ball to diameter length. Thus, a six-inch ball would be inflated to six inches in diameter, and an eight-inch ball would be inflated to eight inches in diameter and so on. These kinds of balls sometimes come in sets ranging from a five-inch ball to a thirteen-inch ball. Although these are the specifications, the teacher can make the ball "faster" (more resilient) by inflating it more or "slower" (less resilient) by inflating it less. Obviously, a slower ball should be easier to handle.

In addition to the various sizes of balls, they sometimes come in a variety of colors. Preschool children are not as likely to be concerned with color as they are with size. At this level the size of a ball should be such that it is easy for a child to visualize it. At kindergarten level color begins to play a part, and by grades one and two *both* color and size are important.

Some years ago our own naturalistic observations of five-year-old identical twin girls—left on their own to select a size and color of ball—yielded some interesting results. Each twin was placed alone with an observer in a separate room and given liberty to select one ball with which to play. The sizes of the balls were five, six, eight, ten and thirteen inches (as measured through the diameter as previously mentioned). Each size of ball came in colors of green, red, blue, orange and yellow. Each of the twins were observed to do essentially the same thing. First, they selected the smallest ball. After playing with this ball for a time (most of the activity involved tapping) there was a direct change to the largest ball. And finally, they settled on the mid-point eight-inch ball.

We theorized that the small ball was selected first, perhaps because little children tend to like little things, such as little tables and chairs, and little dishes. Upon having difficulty in manipulating the five-inch ball, the move was then made to the large ball probably because it had "more room on it" and could be more easily handled. After a reasonable degree of success, such as with tapping, the final selection was the eight-inch ball.

The final color decided upon by each twin was yellow. This was counter to most color preference studies which tend to show that blue is the most popular color and yellow the least popular.

Specialized

Examples of specialized media for perceptual-motor training used in two different programs will be presented here. These are the Perceptual-Motor Training Laboratory, which is a part of the movement education program for children at Purdue University, mentioned previously, and the Children's Physical Developmental Clinic at the University of Maryland.

The objectives of the perceptual-motor area of the Purdue program are stated as follows by the Coordinator, Dr. Marguerite Clifton:[28]

1. To provide an opportunity for the child to develop a more realistic concept of his own body size and the amount of space that his body will require in the performance of varied movement activities.

---

[28] Clifton, Marguerite, *op. cit.* p. 36.

2. To encourage the child to seek experiences which require him to process varied sensory information (auditory, tactual, proprioceptive, visual) in order to refine gross motor tasks.

A series of 17 perceptual training tasks have been devised, and each emphasizes the use of a particular perceptual mode, but not always to the exclusion of other modalities. Each of the tasks utilizes an original piece of equipment designed specifically for this program. Accomplishment of a given task requires a child to employ the appropriate perceptual modality or combination of modalities.

The "bedspring walk" is an example of one piece of equipment in which the child is required to attend to proprioceptive input in order to accomplish any one of several tasks, and particularly when his eyes are closed. The equipment is simply a double set of old-fashioned bed springs covered with canvas. (Specifications of the equipment used to accomplish the various tasks have been published by Jacqueline Herkowitz).[29]

The final example of specialized perceptual-motor media reported here is that which has been designed and developed by Dr. Warren R. Johnson, Director of the Children's Physical Developmental Clinic at the University of Maryland. These media are produced by Medical Motovation Systems, Inc., Research Park, State Road, Princeton, New Jersey under the name of *NPO Equipment* (Neuromuscular Perceptual Organization).

The equipment consists of the NPO Balance Beam, NPO Kick-Throw Rebounder and NPO Footprint Guide, the first of which will be described here.

The NPO Balance Beam beckons the learner forward. The child steps onto the lighted starting target, thereby causing the first panel or target of the balance beam to light up. Each target is different in color and each successful step causes the next one to light—inviting the child to the next correct move. This beckoning technique has been found to hold the attention even of

[29] Herkowitz, Jacqueline: A perceptual-motor train'ng program to improve the gross motor abilities of preschoolers. *Journal of Health, Physical Education, and Recreation,* April, 1970, pp. 38–42.

individuals of diagnosed short attention span—to achieve repetition of effort and to create rapid progress in balance and coordination. Completion of the balanced walk brings an acknowl-
edging buzzer to signal success and reward the effort. The task
may be made more difficult by simply turning the beam over to
its narrower side. And, it is possible to measure progress in the
time needed to accomplish the task and in correctness of walking, either forward or backward.

A film with children actually using the equipment is available
to assist in the training of aides and volunteers who supervise
children. The objectives of using NPO Equipment are explained
and a variety of uses for each unit are shown.

It is appropriate in closing this chapter to reemphasize caution and restraint in the use of perceptual-motor training. While
under adequate supervision and with properly prepared personnel, many of the types of experiences alluded to in the
chapter can be of value. Nevertheless, the "bandwagon" syndrome connected with any relatively new approach to dealing
with behavior of children needs to be taken into account.

CHAPTER FIVE

DEVELOPING READING SKILLS THROUGH MOTOR ACTIVITIES[1]

ACTIVE GAMES ARE one aspect of motor activities. The important role of play and games in cognition and learning has been recognized for centuries. In fact, the idea of the playing of games as a desirable learning medium has been traced to the ancient Egyptians. Through the ages some of the most profound thinkers in history have expounded positively in terms of the value of games as a way of learning. Perhaps one of the earliest pronouncements in this regard was Plato's suggestion that" . . . in teaching children; train them by a kind of game and you will be able to see more clearly the natural bent of each."

In modern times there has been a revival of the *play way* of learning among some educators and psychologists. Much of this has tended to center around certain educational games more or less *passive* in nature. The approach in this chapter is concerned essentially with those types of games which are *active* in nature. Therefore, throughout the chapter the term *games* will imply *active interaction of children in cooperative and/or competitive situations.* In other words, when we speak of active games as a learning medium, we refer to things that children *do* actively in a pleasurable social situation in order to learn. This concept of active games is in agreement with the basic educational principle that learning is always an individual matter, but that it takes most effectively in a social setting. Two important aspects con-

[1] Material for this chapter has been adapted from: Humphrey, James H., and Sullivan, Dorothy D.: *Teaching Slow Learners Through Active Games.* Springfield, Illinois: Charles C Thomas, Publisher, 1970.

cerned with this principle are that (a) a group can stimulate individual activity, and (b) individuals in a group can learn vicariously from each other. Active games provide an outstanding setting for this type of situation.

As indicated in Chapter One, the procedure of learning through active games involves the selection of an active game which is taught to the children and used as a learning activity for the development of a skill or concept. An attempt is made to arrange an active learning situation so that a fundamental intellectual skill or concept is being developed or practiced in the course of participating in the active game. Activities are selected on the basis of the skill or concept involved as well as the appropriate physical ability and social level of a given group of children.

In the active-game approach, a theory of learning that is accepted is that learning takes place in terms of reorganization of the systems of perception into a functional and integrated whole because of the result of certain stimuli. This implies that problem solving is the way of human learning and that learning takes place through problem solving. In an active game learning situation that is well planned, a great deal of consideration will be given to the inherent possibilities for learning in terms of problem solving. In fact, in most active games, opportunities abound for near-ideal teaching-learning situations because there are many problems to be solved. The following sample comments by children indicate that there is a great opportunity for reflective thinking, use of judgment, and problem solving in the active game experience.

1. Would two circles be better than one?
2. You really have to listen carefully to hear the number of syllables in the words.
3. I need to look at the words carefully so I won't make mistakes.
4. Let's make the game harder by saying whether the vowel in the word is long or short.

The active game approach to learning is also concerned with other elements that are inherent in the participation of active games. Three such elements involve *motivation,* particularly as it relates to interest, *proprioception,* and certain principles of *reinforcement.*

FACTORS INFLUENCING LEARNING THROUGH MOTOR ACTIVITY

Motivation

In considering motivation as an inherent facilitative factor of learning in the active game approach, we would like to think of the term in the same manner as it is described in the *Dictionary of Education:*

> . . . the practical art of applying incentives and arousing interest for the purpose of causing a pupil to perform in' a desired way; usually designates the act of choosing study materials of such a sort and presenting them in such a way that they appeal to the pupil's interests and cause him to attack the work at hand willingly and to complete it with sustained enthusiasm; also designates the use of various devices such as the offering of rewards or an appeal to the desire to excel.[2]

We need also take into account *extrinsic and intrinsic* motivation. Extrinsic motivation is described as "the application of incentives that are external to a given activity to make work palatable and to facilitate performance, for example, offering a prize to the pupil who makes the highest score in a spelling test as an appeal to the extrinsic desire to excel." Intrinsic motivation is the "determination of behavior that is resident within an activity and that sustains it, as with autonomous acts and interests."[3]

Extrinsic motivation has been and continues to be used as a means of spurring individuals to achievement. This most often takes the form of various kinds of reward incentives. The main objection to this type of motivation is that it tends to focus the learner's attention upon the reward rather than the learning task and the total learning situation.

In general, the child is motivated when he discovers what

[2] Good, Carter V.: Dictionary of Education, 2nd ed. New York, McGraw-Hill, Inc., 1959, p. 354.
[3] *Ibid.*

seems to him to be a suitable reason for engaging in a certain activity. The most valid reason of course is that he sees a purpose for the activity and derives enjoyment from it. The child must feel that what he is doing is important and purposeful. When this occurs and the child gets the impression that he is being successful in a group situation, the motivation is intrinsic, since it comes about naturally as a result of the child's interest in the activity. It is the premise here that the active game approach contains this "built-in" ingredient so necessary to desirable and worthwhile learning.

The ensuing discussions of this section of the chapter will be concerned with three aspects of motivation that are considered to be inherent in the active game learning medium. These are (a) motivation in relation to *interest*, (b) *motivation in relation to knowledge of results*, and (c) motivation in relation to *competition*.

Motivation in Relation to Interest

It is important to have an understanding of the meaning of interest as well as an appreciation of how interests function as an adjunct to learning. As far as the meaning of the term is concerned, the following description given some time ago by Lee and Lee expresses in a relatively simple manner what is meant by the terms *interest* and *interests:* "*Interest* is a state of being, a way of reacting to a certain situation. *Interests* are those fields or areas to which a child reacts with interest consistently over an extended period of time."[4]

There is a principle of learning that suggests that "learning takes place best when the child agrees with and acts upon the learning which he considers of most value to him."[5] This means that the child accepts as most valuable those things that are of greatest interest to him. To the very large majority of children, their active play experiences are of the greatest personal value to them.

---

[4] Lee, J. Murray, and Lee, Dorris May: *The Child and His Development.* New York, Appleton-Century-Crofts, 1958, p. 382.

[5] Humphrey, James H.: *Child Learning Through Elementary School Physical Education.* Dubuque, Iowa, William C. Brown Co., 1966, p. 109.

Under most circumstances a very high interest level is concomitant with active game situations simply because of the expectation of pleasure children tend to associate with such activities. The structure of a learning activity is directly related to the length of time the learning act can be tolerated by the learner without loss of interest. Active game situations by their very nature are more likely to be so structured than many of the traditional learning activities.

Motivation in Relation to Knowledge of Results

Knowledge of results is most commonly referred to as *feedback*. It was suggested by Brown many years ago that feedback is the process of providing the learner with information as to how accurate his reactions were.[6] Ammons has referred to feedback as knowledge of various kinds which the performer received about his performance.[7]

It has been reported by Bilodeau and Bilodeau that knowledge of results is the strongest, most important variable controlling performance and learning, and further that studies have repeatedly shown that there is no improvement without it, progressive improvement with it, and deterioration after its withdrawal.[8] As a matter of fact, there appears to be a sufficient abundance of objective evidence that indicates that learning is usually more effective when one receives some immediate information on how he is progressing. It would appear rather obvious that such knowledge of results is an important adjunct to learning because one would have little idea of which of his responses were correct. Dolinsky makes the analogy that it would be like trying to learn a task while blindfolded.[9]

[6] Brown, J.S.: A proposed program of research on psychological feedback (knowledge of results) in the performance of psychomotor tasks. Research Planning Conference on Perceptual and Motor Skills, AFHRRC Conf. Rept. 1949, U.S. Air Force, San Antonio, Texas. pp. 1–98.

[7] Ammons, R.B.: Effects of knowledge of performance: A survey and tentative theoretical formulation. *Journal of General Psychology*, LIV: 279–99, 1956.

[8] Bilodeau, Edward A., and Bilodeau, Ina: Motor skill learning. *Annual Review of Psychology*, Palo Alto, Calif., 1961, pp. 243–70.

[9] Dolinsky, Richard: *Human Learning*. Dubuque, Iowa, William C. Brown Co., 1966, p. 13.

The active game approach to learning provides almost instan-
taneous knowledge of results because the child can actually *see
and feel* himself throw a ball, or tag, or be tagged in a game. He
does not become the victim of a poorly constructed paper and
pencil activity in which the tasks involved may have little or no
meaning for him. This is particularly important as far as the
slower learning child is concerned.

Motivation in Relation to Competition

In discussing competition as a factor of motivation it is essential to consider the nature of active games as presented at the
beginning of the chapter, that of *active interaction of children in
cooperative and/or competitive situations.* It is possible to have
both cooperation and competition functioning at the same time,
as in the case of team games. While one team is competing
against the other, there is cooperation within each group. It is
also possible to have one group competing against another without cooperation within the groups. An example of this type of
game is Steal the Bacon described in Chapter Two.

It is interesting to note that the terms *cooperation* and *competition* are antonymous; therefore, the reconciliation of children's
competitive needs and cooperative needs is not an easy matter.
In a sense we are confronted with an ambivalent condition,
which if not carefully handled could place children in a state of
conflict. Horney recognized this many years ago when she stated:

> On the one hand everything is done to spur us toward success,
> which means that we must be not only assertive but aggressive,
> able to push others out of the way. On the other hand we are
> deeply imbued with Christian ideals which declare that it is selfish
> to want anything for ourselves, that we should be humble, turn
> the other hand, be yielding.[10]

Thus our modern society not only rewards one kind of behavior
(competition) but also its direct opposite (cooperation). Perhaps more often than not our cultural demands sanction these
rewards without provision of clear-cut standards of value with
regard to specific conditions under which these forms of behavior

[10] Horney, Karen: *The Neurotic Personality of Our Time.* New York, Norton,
1937.

might well be practiced. Hence, the child is placed in somewhat of a quandary with reference to when to compete and when to cooperate.

In generalizing on the basis of the available evidence with regard to the subject of competition, it appears justifiable to formulate the following concepts:

1. Very young children in general are not very competitive but become more so as they get older.
2. There is a wide variation in competition among children; that is, some are violently competitive while others are mildly competitive, and still others are not competitive at all.
3. Boys tend to be more competitive than girls.
4. Competition should be adjusted so that there is not a preponderant number of winners over losers.
5. Competition and rivalry produce results in effort and speed of accomplishment.

In the school situation teachers might well be guided by the above concepts. As far as active games are concerned, they not only appear to be a good medium for learning because of the intrinsic motivation inherent in them, but also this medium of learning can provide for competitive needs of children in a pleasurable and enjoyable way.

Proprioception

Earlier in this chapter it was stated that the theory of learning accepted here is that learning takes place in terms of a reorganization of the systems of perception into a functional and integrated whole as a result of certain stimuli. These sensory systems of perception, or sensory processes as they are sometime referred to, not only consist of the senses of sight, hearing, touch, smell, and taste but also muscle sense, this latter process by which information is fed to the human organism, known as *proprioception*, was previously mentioned in Chapter Two. It seems reasonable to speculate that proprioceptive feedback from the receptors of muscles, skin, and joints contributes in a facilitative manner when the active game learning medium is used to develop academic skills and concepts. The combination of the psychological factor of motivation and the physiological factor of proprioception inherent in the active game approach to learning has caused us to coin the term *motorvation* to describe this phenomenon.

Credence has been given to the old Chinese proverb that "one picture is worth a thousand words." Another Chinese proverb extends the dimension of the learning process, "I hear, and I forget. I see, and I remember. I do, and I understand." In modern times we need to give consideration to the possibility of *muscle use* for learning as being worth a thousand pictures.

Reinforcement

In considering the compatibility of the active-game learning medium with reinforcement theory, the meaning of reinforcement needs to be taken into account. An acceptable general description of reinforcement would be that there is an increase in the efficiency of a response to a stimulus brought about by the concurrent action of another stimulus. The basis for contending that the active game-learning medium is consistent with *general* reinforcement theory is that this medium reinforces attention to the learning task and learning behavior. It keeps children involved in the learning activity, which is perhaps the major area of application for reinforcement procedures. While speaking basically of *passive* rather than *active* games for remedial reading instruction Wilson states that "games can provide the reinforcement needed for the overlearning of skills without the negative aspects of routine monotonous drill."[11] Wilson cites the use of games for skills development of auditory and visual discrimination, word attack, vocabulary, and problem solving.

As reported in the "reinforcement" study in Chapter Two it would appear that the active game-learning medium generally establishes a more effective situation for learning reinforcement for the following reasons: First, the greater motivation of the children in the active game learning situation involves accentua-

[11] Wilson, Robert M.: *Diagnostic and Remedial Reading for Classroom and Clinic,* 2nd ed. Columbus, Charles E. Merrill, 1972, p. 206.

tion of those behaviors directly pertinent to their learning activities, making these salient for the purpose of reinforcement. Second, the proprioceptive emphasis in active game learning involves a greater number of *responses* associated with and conditioned to learning stimuli. And finally, the gratifying aspects of the active game situations provide a generalized situation of *reinforcers*.

It is recognized, despite the present authors' extolling the "learning" values of the active games approach, that this approach has its limitations. It should be pointed out very forcefully here that we recognize it as *another* valid way that children might learn, and not necessarily the only way. We are well aware of the fact that everything cannot be taught best through active games, simply because all children do not learn in the same way. But there is pretty general agreement that the premise of active games as a learning medium is sound from all standpoints: philosophical, physiological, and psychological.

USING ACTIVE GAMES FOR READING INSTRUCTION

Active games in reading instruction can serve two basic purposes. Some games can be particularly useful for developing specific language or reading concepts. In these games the learner acts out the concept and thus is able to visualize as well as get the *feel* of the concept. Other games help to develop skills through reinforcement of these skills in highly interesting and stimulating situations. Such active games can be utilized effectively to develop skills in the areas of *sight vocabulary, word analysis skills* (letter recognition, auditory and visual discrimination, auditory-visual association, vowel letter patterns, syllabication, affixes, accent, alphabetical order), *comprehension* (following directions, classification, vocabulary meaning, sequence of events).

In working with the active games approach to teach reading skills, several guidelines can be useful to the teacher in order to provide meaningful and satisfying experiences for children. Often, games can be set up with the entire class participating. In such cases it is important that the less able reader not be penalized for his slowness or inability to perform a given task by being eliminated from the game. Rules of the game can employ procedures to incorporate a buddy-system for giving responses or points earned for the individual or team. Such procedures provide the slower learner the practice he needs by him remaining in the game and yet does not hamper the rest of the children in their competitive efforts to win.

In some games the children are divided into teams. In such situations it is considered a wise practice for the teacher to arrange the selection method so that there is a balance of able readers as well as less able readers assigned to each team. This should also be considered when different physical skills are called for in a specific game. Such arranging by the teacher need not appear obvious and does help to provide a satisfying experience for all the children with a more even competition.

The teacher may also elect to use a game for one particular group of children. This is appropriate when only one group within the class needs additional work with a given skill, and to include all children would make the less able children feel inadequate and bore those children who have mastered the skill.

After a game has been played, it should be evaluated not only in terms of the children's reaction to the game and how it was played, but also in terms of how well the children understand the concepts inherent in the game, that is, what specific reading skill they were practicing. The game situation can also serve as a means of evaluating specific skill needs of children in terms of planning further instruction.

The following illustration describes an active game that demonstrates the first type of active game mentioned above, that of developing a concept that is inherent in the activity itself.[12] The game facilitates the understanding of certain vocabulary words through the activities of the game. There had been some previous experiences with the meaning of these words as well as auditory, and for some children, visual recognition of the words and the concept of "opposites."

Concept: Vocabulary Meaning - Word Opposites

---

[12] Humphrey, Sullivan, *op. cit.* pp. 87–88. There are over fifty games classified according to the major areas of reading skills.

Activity: I'm Tall, I'm Small

The children form a circle with one child in the center. The child in the center of the circle stands with his eyes closed. It may be helpful to have the child blindfolded. The children in the circle walk slowly around the circle singing or saying the following verse:

I'm tall, I'm very small,
I'm small, I'm very tall,
Sometimes I'm tall,
Sometimes I'm small,
Guess what I am now.

As the children walk and sing "tall," "very tall," or "small," "very small," they stretch up or stoop down, depending on the words. At the end of the singing the teacher signals the children in the circle to assume a stretching or stooping position. The child in the center, still with eyes closed, guesses which position they have taken. For the next game another child is selected to be in the center.

Application:

This activity helps children to develop word meaning by acting out the words. Use of word opposites in this manner helps to dramatize the differences in the meaning of words. The words and actions can be changed to incorporate a larger number of "opposites," for example:

My hands are near, my hands are far.
Now they're far, now they're near.
Sometimes they're near.
Sometimes they're far.
Guess what they are now.

Teaching Procedure:

Teacher: Boys and girls, do you remember the other day we were talking about things that were tall and things that were small? What are some of the things we found at school that were tall? (Children) Very good. Can you think of some things we thought were small? (Children) Can you remember some things we decided were sometimes tall and sometimes small? (Children) That's right. We said trees could be tall and small. And we said people were both tall and small. Who in your family is tall? (Children) And who is small? (Children) Very good. Today we are going to play a game called "I'm Tall, I'm Small." We are going to need to remember what the words "tall" and "small" mean in order to play our game. (The teacher goes over the procedures and answers any questions the children may have. The children move to the playing area and proceed with the game. During the game the teacher may make comments.) Make sure you stretch really tall, now, boys and girls. Stretch tall like George Giraffe° did in our story the other day. Some of you need to get down lower when you stoop. And be sure to watch my signal at the end of the song so you will all do the same thing. All right. Let's continue. (Children play game.)

The activity continues for a time, and then the teacher evaluates with the class. Teacher: What did you like best about the game?
(Children) Is it easier to remember what the word "tall" means?
(Children) What do you think of when someone says the word "tall"?
(Children) How about the word "small"? What do you think of?
(Children) How did the game help you remember what each word means?
(Children) How could we improve our playing the game?
(Children) Yes, you have to watch me closely so you'll carry out the right signal. Next time we play the game I'm going to use the word cards saying "tall" and "small" instead of signaling with my hands.† Do you think you could read the words so you would know whether to stretch or to stoop? (Children) Good. Will that be fun to try? (Children)

The next illustration describes an active game to reinforce a specific skill that had been previously introduced.[13] The teacher

---

° See story of George Giraffe in Chapter Six.

† In this case the teacher will be using visual input instead of auditory input.

[13] *Ibid.* p. 70.

can use this game for a group of children to practice their skills of identifying words presented visually with inflectional endings.

Concept: Inflectional Endings - *s, ed, ing*
Activity: Ending Relay

The class is divided into teams. Each team is given a box filled with sight vocabulary words having *s, ed,* and *ing* endings. The boxes are placed by the blackboard. The teams make rows at a starting line ten to fifteen feet from the blackboard. On a signal the first child of each team runs to the team's box and picks out three words, one with an *s* ending, one with *ed,* and one with *ing* ending. He places the words along the chalk tray, pronounces each, and returns to his team. The second child continues in the same manner. If a child is having difficulty, he may call upon one member of his team to help him.* The team that finishes with the accurate selection and pronunciation of words first wins.

Application:

This game enables children to practice their skills in identifying visually presented words with different inflectional endings. The game may later include words with irregular endings. This activity also provides reinforcement of sight vocabulary.

Teaching Procedure:

Teacher: Boys and girls, while the rest of the class is in the library working on their reports we are going to play a game. Do you remember our discussion the other day about having to look carefully at the endings of words? (Children) What word endings were we talking about? (Children) Why is it important to use correct endings? (Children) Yes, they certainly do affect the meanings of words. What does an *s* ending do to the meaning of a word? An *ed* ending? And *ing?* (Children) Very good. Each ending plays an important part in meanings of words.

That is what our game is about today. The game is called Ending Relay. We are going to need to pay close attention to the endings on words in order to play the game. (The teacher goes

---

* There is sufficient evidence to support the idea that in the buddy system both children benefit in the learning task.

over the procedures and answers any questions the children may have. The children proceed with the game. During the game the teacher may make comments.) Remember to select only one word for each ending. Don't forget to pronounce each word you pick. If you need help ask a buddy on your team to help you. Alright. Let's continue. (Children play game.)

The activity continues for a time, and then the teacher evaluates with the class. Teacher: What did you like best about the game? (Children) Are you better able to read endings correctly? (Children) What did you have to do to read the endings of words correctly? (Children) Can anyone think of another way this game helped him in reading? (Children) That's very good. It's easier to remember the words. Yes. Every time we see a word and recognize it, it makes it easier the next time we see the word to be able to read it. Does anyone remember what we call words that we can recognize instantly? (Children) Very good. Yes, we are building our sight vocabulary. How might we improve our playing of the game? (Children) All right, we'll try that the next time we play Ending Relay.

DEVELOPING ACTIVE GAMES FOR READING INSTRUCTION

In developing active games for reading instruction several criteria should be used. The first guideline is using the definition of active games as presented earlier in the chapter. Active games are those in which there is active interaction of children in cooperative and/or competitive situations.

The second guideline is developing a game that appropriately develops a concept or provides repetitive drill for development of specific reading skills. In so doing, the teacher must identify the specific skill to be reinforced in behavioral terms in order to develop a game so the tasks involved are ones that have been introduced previously and in which the child can experience a measure of success. The teacher should identify whether the game being developed has specific concepts inherent in the activity itself (as in "I'm Tall, I'm Small") or if its function is to provide interesting and stimulating settings for developing skills through practice and repetition of these skills.

A third guideline should be the consideration of the appropriateness of the basic motor tasks utilized in the game in terms of the fundamental skill development of the children involved. Types of basic locomotor skills for different age levels that teachers might use in developing games are identified in the following chapter. There is also concern for the complexity of the tasks involved in the game. Some games are simply too complicated in terms of rules to appeal to any but the more able learner. Games should be developed in which the inherent concept is obvious enough and simple enough that most children can participate in the game with enjoyment under proper guidance by the teacher.

In developing active games for reading instruction the teacher therefore considers (1) if children's needs are being met, (2) how well the games are suited to the reading program's objectives, (3) if there is a balanced program in terms of a variety of types of activities in the games developed, and (4) if the activities can be adapted to the group's needs. It has been found that many games can be adapted to numerous skills and levels of difficulty by altering the tasks involved in the game. Creative teachers have found the versatility that is possible in adapting games to various aspects of the reading program.

CHAPTER SIX

MOTOR-ORIENTED READING CONTENT

BASIC FACTS ABOUT the nature of human beings serve educators today as principles of learning. One of these principles, *that learning takes place best when the child has his own purposeful goals to guide his learning activities,* serves as the basis for developing motor-oriented reading content material. Generally speaking, there are two ways in which motor-oriented reading content can be developed. These are through the *language experience stories* of children and *prepared stories.*

THE LANGUAGE EXPERIENCE STORIES OF CHILDREN

The language experience approach (LEA) can very effectively involve children developing group or individual stories based on active games they have learned to play. This technique involves the usual procedures of the children first discussing important aspects of their experience in order for their stories to be detailed and accurate enough that other children could read their story and be able to play the game. Such aspects of reading as sufficient detail and accuracy of information plus correct sequencing of procedures involves many higher-level cognitive aspects of problem solving.

After the discussion the children begin to dictate their story about how to play the game which the teacher records on the board or on large chart paper. It is important that the language patterns of children be recorded intact. The teacher records the words exactly as the children dictate them but spelling the words correctly. The teacher uses guided questioning to help children put in sufficient details and proper sequence in the procedures for playing the game in their story. After the children have dictated their story they may reread it to be sure it has enough information so that others are able to play the game after reading their story. The children may even play the game again to be sure they have all the necessary steps. The language experience story based on such a physically-oriented activity facilitates the concept that the printed word symbols represent not only their oral language, but also these words (both oral and printed) represent things that they do, see, feel, and think about.

Once the story has been developed the teacher prepares a copy of the story on large chart paper (if the story was originally recorded on the board) and makes sufficient dittoed copies for each child to keep his own copy of the story, several copies for each child (to be used later for skill development activities), and one copy for a class book of games. Individual words, phrases, sentences from the stories are printed on oak tag strips.

The copy of the story on large chart paper is used for teacher-directed group or individual instruction for developing the following reading skills:

(a) sight vocabulary (by rereading stories; visual matching of word, phrase, sentence cards; and collecting words for children's word banks)

(b) word attack skills and their application to context reading (by "word hunts" for words in story that have the same word attack pattern previously learned while working with individual words in isolation

(c) Comprehension skills of vocabulary meaning, sequence, inference, and problem solving.

The children can also help to make the class book of their game-stories by making illustrations for the book. The book can then be bound and made available for children to read on their own by putting it in the classroom or school library. Some children might even want to make up new games and write stories about them.

An example of such an activity by which children developed their own motor-oriented reading content stories took place in a third grade classroom.[1] The particular reading activity was an outgrowth of a social studies unit concerned with the community and people who contribute to a community's welfare. Among the various community helpers studied, the duties of a policeman seemed to be quite fascinating. This particular class consisted largely of a low third-grade group reading on first- and second-grade instructional level. The teacher introduced a new game about a policeman to the children and the class dictated a story about the way the new game was to be played. After rereading the story several times the children played the game.

A second story was written after the children had played the new game. This story was done by a remedial group of children reading on a first-grade level. In a remarkably short time, each child in the group was able to read the entire story quite fluently. Reading skill activities included those mentioned above. Reading in this particular instance was fun and something which each child could do with relatively little difficulty. It was a new experience for several in the group because reading from the basal text was difficult for them. One child reported that he "read it all for the first time." The teacher observed that this type of activity-experience story offered innumerable opportunities for a good developmental-reading lesson. She noticed that the interest appeal was high and the amount of individual success was very gratifying to each child.

PREPARED STORIES

One of the early and perhaps the first attempt to prepare motor-oriented reading content as conceived here is the work of Humphrey and Moore.[2] Their original work involved a detailed study of reactions of six-to-eight-year-old children when independent reading material is oriented to active game participation. This experiment was initiated on the premise of relating reading content for children to their natural urge to play.

[1] Humphrey, James H., *Child Learning Through Elementary School Physical Education.* Dubuque, Iowa, William C. Brown, Co., 1966, p. 154.

[2] Humphrey, James H., and Moore, Virginia D.: Improving reading through physical education. *Education* (The Reading Issue), 559, May, 1960.

The original study utilizing games written with a story setting has been described in Chapter Two. From this study additional stories were developed along the same criteria as the original stories and published as the Read and Play series.[3] This series consists of six books in which there are 131 stories. Set One of the Series is for First Grade and Set Two is for Second Grade. Each set consists of three books. The stories in the first two books in each set are written around active games or stunt settings. And the third book in each set is written around a rhythmic or dance setting.

This carefully developed material—in terms of readability, the reading values, and literary merit of the stories—utilizes children's natural affinity for motor-oriented play as the motivation for their reading. This unique reading content calls for active responses to the reading task, the task being one that involves learning to play an active game or to perform physically-oriented stunts or rhythms. Such tasks bring a physical reality to printed word symbols.

Motor-oriented reading content material, while enriching and extending the childs experiences reinforces his general ability to read through his reading independently and "on his own." A child or group of children may read a story individually, in buddy teams, or as a group with the teacher providing individual help with words when needed. After reading the story the child or children play the game or perform the stunt or rhythm activity. They may then reread the story and discuss how they might improve upon their first attempt at carrying out the motor-oriented task. With this procedure the child is able to develop cognitive processing skills through the physical reality of the activity involved. The child is therefore provided opportunities to practice and maintain skills necessary for meaningful reading.

A further dimension of the stories such as in the Read and Play approach is the purpose setting and problem-solving nature inherent in the reading activities of the stories. The child is

---

[3] Humphrey, James H., and Moore, Virginia D.: *Read and Play Series*. Garrard Publishing Co., Champaign, Illinois, 1962. Selected for publication by Frederick Muller, Limited, London, England, 1965.

reading to find out how to do something—play a game or do a stunt. The child is using all his skills in reading to solve the problem of performing the task described in the story. Both purpose-setting and problem-solving have been identified as essential to the higher cognitive processes in mature reading. Such reading activities as the Read and Play approach can provide children their first opportunities to exercise these skills with physically real experiences.

Furthermore, this approach enables the teacher to assess the child's vocabulary development and how well comprehension skills are being practiced because the children actually demonstrate their understanding of what they read. Thus, the teacher can observe by their actions the children's comprehension of the material. This relates closely with Chapter Eight's use of motor-oriented learning activities as a means of diagnosing skills in reading.

Introducing the Material

After the prepared stories have been made available for the classroom library the teacher may introduce several stories by reading them to the children and then having the children play the game or demonstrate the stunt or rhythm. Stories developing each type of physical activity should be selected so children will understand how the stories provide details they can use to figure out how to perform a stunt or rhythmic activity or to play a game. Sample stories should also be selected to demonstrate that some stories can be acted out by an individual child and that some require several children to participate in the stunt or game. This latter aspect of the motor-oriented reading content material utilizes another basic principle of learning, *that learning takes place best when the child is given the opportunity to share cooperatively in learning experiences with his classmates* (under the guidance but not the control of the teacher.) The point that should be emphasized here is that, although learning may be an individual matter, it is likely to take place best in a group. This is to say that children learn individually but that socialization should be retained. Moreover, sharing in group activities seems an absolute essential in educating for democracy.

After the teacher reads a sample story the children are asked to carry out the activity. As the children carry out the activity the teacher *accepts* their efforts. The teacher may provide guidance *only* to the extent it is necessary to help the children identify problems and provide opportunity for them to exercise judgment in solving them and obtaining their goal, that of playing the game or performing the stunt or rhythm. Parts of the story might be reread by the teacher if the children have difficulty in understanding how to carry out the activity. The children might be encouraged to discuss ways they could help themselves remember the details of the story—by pretending they are Casper Camel or Grizzly Bear or that they were really playing the game, that they might take more time and read more carefully so they can recall details better.

Independent Reading and Follow-Up Play Activities

After such an introduction to the prepared stories the children should be encouraged to read them "on their own." The teacher and children might plan several procedures for using the stories. Such activities might include:

(1) A group of children may select and read a story for a physical education activity.

(2) Individual children may select stories involving individual stunts for a physical education period.

(3) After reading one of the Read and Play books an individual child may elect to act out his favorite stunt story before a group of children. (The children might be asked to guess who or what the story describes.)

(4) After reading one of the stories an individual might get several other children to read the story and participate in playing the game.

(5) Children might use a buddy system for reading and acting out stories.

(6) Children might write and illustrate similar-type stories for other children to read and act out.

The following are specific suggestions for procedures that might be utilized in working with the basic types of stories that appear in the Read and Play series, group games, individual stunts, and rhythms.

In the first situation during which a group of children are to play a game after having read the story "Wilbur Woodchuck and His Cane,"[4] the teacher might direct the following discussion before the children attempt to play the game:

Wilbur Woodchuck and His Cane

Wilbur Woodchuck hurt his leg.
He needed a walking stick.
At last his leg got better.
He did not need his stick.
He said, "I will find some friends.
We will play a game with my stick."
Wilbur's friends stood in line.
Wilbur was in front of the line.
He stood the stick in front of him.
He held it with his hand.
He called a friend's name.
Wilbur let the stick fall.
His friend caught it
    before it hit the ground.
He took Wilbur's place.
They played for a long time.
Could you find something to use for a stick
and play this game with other children?

Teacher: How is Wilbur Woodchuck's game played? (Children) Do we need any specific thing in order to play the game? (Children) Good. What can we use for Wilbur's cane? (Children) That's a good idea to use a yardstick since we don't have a cane. Now, where might be a good place to mark the line? (Children) Alright, Allan you may mark the line. And since you selected the story you may be the first one to be Wilbur. Where does Wilbur stand? (Children) Where do his friends stand? (Children) The rest of you may take your place along the line as Wilbur's friends. (The game is played.)

Following the activity the teacher helps the children to eval-

---

[4] *Ibid.*, Set 1, Book 2, p. 18.

uate: What were some of the things you liked about the game? (Children) What difficulty did you have in playing the game? (Children) Yes, the yardstick did seem hard to catch when it was falling. Perhaps one of you may have a cane at home that you could loan us so we could play the game better. Some of you didn't seem to know what to do when the person does not catch the cane before it falls to the ground. What could we do to find out? (Children) Good. Let's read the story again to make sure what we are to do. (Children reread.) What does the story say to do? (Children) Then how do we know what to do? (Children) That is very good, boys and girls. Sometimes we have to "infer" from what we read. How can we help ourselves to recognize these inferences? (Children) You mentioned that you enjoyed the game. Can you remember why Wilbur Woodchuck decided to make up a game? (Children) What might be another name for this game? (Children)

In a situation during which children are taking turns acting out their favorite stunt story the teacher might direct the following discussion after a child's presentation of "George Giraffe:[5]

George Giraffe

There is a tall animal in a far away land.
He has a long neck.
His name is George Giraffe.
You could look like him if you did this.
Place your arms high over your head.
Put your hands together.
Point them to the front.
This will be his neck and head.
Now walk like George Giraffe.
This is how.
Stand on your toes.
Walk with your legs straight.
Could you walk so you would look
    like George Giraffe?

Teacher: Wasn't that interesting the way Johnny showed us how George Giraffe looked? (Children) What do you think George Giraffe looked like from what Johnny did? (Children) What did Johnny do to look tall like George Giraffe? What

[5] *Ibid.* Set 1, Book 1, p. 30.

did Johnny do to have a long neck like George Giraffe? (Children) Can someone else make a long neck? (Children demonstrate.) Oh, you are *all* very good at making long necks. Particularly Jimmy. How did Johnny walk to be like George Giraffe? Can someone show me? (Children demonstrate.) What do you have to do to walk like a giraffe? (Children) Is it easy to pretend to be a giraffe? Let's try it and find out. (All children demonstrate.) Did you feel awkward? (Children) We often say that giraffes look "ungainly" or "awkward." Do you think these are good words to describe a giraffe? (Children) Can you think of other words we might use to describe a giraffe? (Children) Can you think of other animals that also look "awkward" or "ungainly"? (Children) That was good, Johnny. You really showed us how to look like a giraffe. You must have read the story very carefully. Bobby, you said you also had read the story about George Giraffe. Why do I say "Johnny must have read very carefully?" (Bobby) That's right. It is important to use all the information the story gives to help you to pretend to be something. That was fun, wasn't it? (Children) Alright. Now Mary is going to tell us about her story. But this time we are going to do it differently. This time Mary is *not* going to tell us the name of her story, or what she is pretending to be. We will have to guess *who* or *what* she is. In this manner the group continues to share, discuss, act out, and evaluate the stories the children present.

In a situation in which children are acting out rhythmic activities after reading a story the teacher might direct the following discussion after the children have read the story "Swinging and Swaying."[6]

Swinging and Swaying

Can you swing and sway to music? Here are new words to "Rock-a-bye, Baby." As you sing the words, can you think of different ways to swing and sway?

Swinging and swaying
Go to and fro.

[6] *Ibid.* Set 2, Book 3, p. 33.

Sway in the breeze
Turn round as you go.
Sway in the breeze
Turn round as you go.
Swinging and swaying
Go to and fro.

Could you do something different with your hands each time you sway to this song?

Teacher: You've selected an interesting story for us today, Mary and Susan. Can you tell us why you chose this one for everyone to read? (Children) Yes, I'm sure most everyone does know the song "Rock-a-bye, Baby." I have it here, let's listen to it. (Children listen.) In our story something about our song has been changed. Can anyone tell me what it is? (Children) What did you think was swinging and swaying in the new words? (Children) You have some good ideas. Let's all swing and sway now as we hear the music. Try to sing along with the new words. (Children) That's a good idea. Let's sing the new words together before we try to swing and sway. But first, let's read them together. (Children) Fine. Are we ready to sing now? (Children) Yes, it is hard not to forget to sing the new words. You did very well. Now, let's swing and sway as we sing. Are we all going to do the same thing? (Children) Good. I'll be interested in seeing how each of you swings and sways in the breeze. (Children sing and demonstrate rhythm.) Very good, boys and girls. How many said they were flowers? (Children) How many of you were trees? (Children) And Johnny, you said you were tall grass in the fields. I could almost see tall grass by the way you were swaying and turning around. What were some of the different things you all did with your hands each time you sway to this song? (Children demonstrate.) Alright. Let's try it again. (Children sing and demonstrate.) I can see some of you were gentle breezes and some of you were almost like a "high wind" in a storm. Who can tell which of you were more a "high wind." (Children) What did they do to be like a "high wind"? (Children) They must really have liked this song. Perhaps we could make up a story about all kinds of winds someday soon.

Developing Prepared Stories by the Teacher

Motor-oriented content stories can be developed by the teacher. This has been successfully done by teachers who have produced amazingly creative stories using games, stunts, and rhythms. Teachers have also involved children in such projects as creative writing experiences. In writing such stories using a motor-activity setting there are several guidelines that the teacher should keep in mind.

In general the new word load should be kept relatively low. There should be as much repetition of these words as possible and appropriate. Sentence length and lack of complexity in sentences should be considered in keeping the level of difficulty of material within the independent reading levels of children. There are numerous readability formulas that can be utilized. For primary-level stories Spache's Readability Formula[7] and MaGinnis' revision of Fry's Readability Graph[8] are best suited. For upper-level stories Fry's Readability Graph is useful.

Consideration must also be given to the reading values and literary merits of the story. Using a character or characters in a story setting helps to develop interest. The game to be used in the story should not be readily identifiable. For example, the game "Catch the Cane" is not immediately evident in the story "Wilbur Woodchuck and His Cane." When children identify a game early in the story there can be resulting minimum attention on the part of the readers to get the necessary details in order to play the game. In developing a game story, therefore, it is important that the nature of the game and procedures of the game unfold gradually.

In developing a game story the equipment, playing area, and procedures should be clearly described. Physical education terminology should be used in describing the game setting. In a *file, row, or column* the children stand one behind the other. In a *line* the children stand beside each other. Basic motor

[7] Spache, George D.: *Good Books for Poor Readers.* Champaign, Illinois, Garrard Publishing Co., 1966. (The Spache Readability Formula was used with the *Read and Play Series.*)

[8] MaGinnis, George H.: The readability graph and informal reading inventories. *The Reading Teacher, 22:*518, March, 1969.

skills that can be utilized in stunt and rhythmic activities as well as for games include *locomotor skills* (walking, running, leaping, jumping, hopping, skipping, galloping, sliding); *throwing and striking skills* (and rolling) with underarm, sidearm, and overarm swing patterns; *catching; and axial movements* (twisting, turning, and stretching). Children should also be given the opportunity to engage in creative rhythms.

Games should be at the developmental level of children. At the primary level games should involve a few simple rules and in some cases elementary strategies. Games that involve chasing and fleeing, tag, and one small group against another, as well as those involving fundamental skills mentioned above are suggested. The games should be simple enough to be easy to learn and they should capitalize upon the imitative and dramatic interests which are typical of this age. (This applies to stunt and rhythmic stories as well.) Children at the upper elementary level retain an interest in some of the games they played at the primary level, and some of them can be extended and made more difficult to meet the needs and interests of these older children. In addition, games may now be introduced which call for greater bodily control, finer coordination of hands, eyes, and feet, and more strength.

In developing games it is also important to strive for maximum activity for all children and avoiding procedures which tend to eliminate players. It may be better to devise some sort of point scoring system than to eliminate a player from the activity when he is tagged in a running game or hit with the ball in a game of dodgeball.

In summary, motor-oriented reading content provides variety to the reading program. High interest and motivation are the results of purposeful reading and bringing words into physical reality by playing a game, performing the stunt, or responding to the rhythm.

CHAPTER SEVEN

LEARNING TO READ
THROUGH CREATIVE MOVEMENT[1]

THERE APPEARS to be rather general agreement on the *intellectual* needs of children. Some of these include (1) a need for challenging experiences at their own level, (2) a need for intellectually successful and satisfying experiences, (3) a need for the opportunity to solve problems, and (4) a need for opportunity to participate in *creative* experiences instead of always having to conform.[2]

For many years now we have been hearing about creativity and giving the child an opportunity to be creative. When a term is used so often and, in fact, in so many different frames of reference, it becomes difficult to completely understand its meaning. For this reason, and for our purpose here we need to identify our meaning of the term as it pertains to the present discussion. We will tend to think of creativity in terms of giving a child his own freedom to respond to perceived situations. This, of course, should be done with various degrees of teacher guidance, inasmuch as children will vary insofar as their ability to be creative is concerned. This is particularly true in the early stages of the more inhibited children.

This line of thought is compatible with a very important prin-

---

[1] Material for this chapter has been adapted from: Wilson, Robert M., Humphrey, James H., and Sullivan, Dorothy D.: *Teaching Reading Through Creative Movement.* The AMAV Technique, Kimbo Educational Records, Deal, New Jersey, 1969. This original work consists of four stories on two long play records, or cassettes, a teacher's manual, and sets of eight booklets of the stories.

[2] Humphrey, James H.: *Child Learning Through Elementary School Physical Education.* Dubuque, Iowa, William C. Brown, Co., 1966, p. 12.

ciple of learning. That is, *desirable learning takes place when the child is free to create his own responses in the situation he faces*.[3] This principle indicates that problem solving is the way of human learning and that the child will learn largely only through experience, either direct or indirect. This implies that the teacher should provide every opportunity for children to utilize judgment in the various perceived situations that arise. It takes the utmost skill on the part of the teacher to know when to "step in and teach," and when to get out of the way and let further learning take place. When the child is free to create his own responses in the situation he faces, individual differences must be taken into consideration.

It is interesting to note that we hear a great deal about the so-called *creative method* and/or the *problem-solving method*. Actually, these might not be methods as such at all, but in reality the application of a valid principle of learning. This is to say that creativity and problem solving should not be isolated as specific methods, but on the contrary they should be involved in all types of methods.

CREATIVITY AND CHILDHOOD

One of the utmost concerns to educators in a modern democratic society is the problem of how to provide for creative expression so that a child may develop to the fullest extent of his potentialities. In fact, democracy is only beginning to understand the *power of the individual* as perhaps the most dynamic force in the world today. It is in this frame of reference that creativity should come clearly into focus because many of the problems in our complex society can be solved only through creative thinking.

Creative experience involves *self* expression. It is concerned with the need to experiment, to express original ideas, to think, to react. Creativity and childhood enjoy a congruous relationship in that children are naturally creative. They imagine. They pretend. They are uninhibited. They are not only original but

[3] *Ibid.* p. 107.

actually ingenious in their thoughts and actions. Indeed, creativity is a characteristic inherent in the lives of practically all children. It may range from some children who create as a natural form of expression without adult stimulation to others who may need varying degrees of teacher guidance and encouragement. School need not stifle the creative nature within children, yet, it often does. Particularly in language do we find teachers inhibiting the child's freedom of response. Again, in the apparent necessity for every child to work quietly in his seat we may find creativity inhibited.

There are a variety of media for creative expression (art, music, and writing) which are considered the traditional approaches to creative expression. However, the very essence of creative expression is *movement*. Movement, as a form of creativity, utilizes the body as the instrument of expression. For the young child, the most natural form of creative expression is movement. Because of their nature, children have a natural inclination for movement and they use this medium as the basic form of creative expression. Movement is the child's universal language, a most important form of communication and a most meaningful way of learning.

THE AMAV TECHNIQUE

The AMAV technique involves a learning sequence of *auditory input* to *movement* to *auditory-visual input as* depicted in Figure 3. Essentially the AMAV technique is a procedure for working through creative movement to develop comprehension first in listening and then in reading. The $A \rightarrow M$ aspect of AMAV is a directed listening-thinking activity. Children first receive the thoughts and feelings expressed in a story through the auditory sense by listening to a recorded story. Following this they engage in movement experiences which are inherent in the story and thereby demonstrate their understanding of

AUDITORY ➡ MOVEMENT ➡ AUDITORY — VISUAL

Figure 3. AMAV Learning Sequence.

and reaction to the story. By engaging in the movement the development of comprehension becomes a part of the child's physical reality. This involves *proprioception* or "muscle sense" described earlier in *Chapter Two*.

After the creative movement experience in the directed listening-thinking activity the children move to the final aspect of the AMAV technique (A–V), a combination of auditory and visual experience by listening to the story and reading along in the story booklet. In this manner comprehension is brought to the reading experience.

Although the comprehension skills for listening and reading are the same, the sensory input is different. That is, listening is dependent upon the auditory sense, and reading is dependent upon the visual sense. The sequence of listening to reading is a natural one. However, bridging the gap to the point of handling the verbal symbols required in reading poses various problems for many children. One of the outstanding features of the AMAV technique is that the movement experience helps to serve as a bridge between listening and reading by providing direct purposeful experience for the child through creative movement after listening to the story.

USES OF THE AMAV TECHNIQUE

The AMAV technique has been implemented through "Teaching Reading Through Creative Movement."[4] The focus of this material is to supplement the reading program with experiences which are varied, creative, and which culminate in movement. Materials for "Teaching Reading Through Creative Movement" (The AMAV Technique) include four recorded story selections on records or cassettes, eight booklets of each of the stories for children to read along as they listen, and a teacher's guide. Prior to publication these materials were tried out extensively with children in various types of educational settings. The creators found them suitable in developmental

4 Wilson, Humphrey, and Sullivan, *op. cit.*, pp. 3–4 of the Teacher's Guide.

programs in grades one and two and in remedial situations in other elementary grades. Children's responses have been enthusiastic and creative.

The basic structure of the Directed-Listening-Thinking Activity in working with each story is the first step of the AMAV technique. The children listen to the story. They act out, talk about, or illustrate their reactions to and their understanding of the story. Later they may use the booklets as they read along with the recording—the final phase of the AMAV technique.

All responses to the stories should be acceptable. Creatively, the child will react in his own way. He must feel like being creative. He must be free to create. His creativity will be limited by his understanding of the story. No criticism should be administered for what the teacher considers to be substandard performance.

Children may work together as they respond. As they work with others they become involved in the creative process and, through movement, become learners. Some children may for their own reasons choose not to become involved in a reaction to the stories. Forcing them to do so will tend to stifle, not generate, creativity. They may be permitted to observe. They should be encouraged but not forced.

For exposure to very young children the first activity might consist of the children listening to and reacting through movement to the stories. Some children may have limited previous experience in expressing themselves through creative dramatics or participation in physical education activities involving imitations of different movements such as the puppy dog run or rabbit jump. They might need some experience such as these. They might also need to move into the stories more slowly. The stories may be presented several times in order to bring out the concepts of the stories and to help children in their interpretation. Later these children may be encouraged to follow the story in their books while listening to it.

The program has particular value when used with seven- and eight-year-old children who are experiencing difficulties in learning to read. Field trials with such children produced extremely rewarding results. The children enjoy the records and read-along books. They tend to find the materials non-threatening and they participate actively.

Procedures for use with slow learning children are the same as those suggested for normal first graders. The children should be permitted to listen to the stories and respond creatively through movement. They should also be permitted to read along with the stories in a second presentation of the selections. If they desire, they should be provided the opportunity to read the stories to others.

Slow learning children will need to have the program paced according to their ability to handle the material. They will need considerable praise for their efforts. It has been found valuable to chart their progress so they can see concrete evidence of their successes. Aside from these few suggestions most children will respond well to the instruction available to normal children.

Of particular value for the slow learning child is the extra reinforcement which comes from the creative movement opportunities. These children often find it difficult to express their understandings in traditional paper and pencil exercises for they cannot spell. They frequently fail to participate in question and answer sessions because they feel inadequate in talking out their ideas.

GUIDELINES[5]

The following are general suggestions for carrying out the directed listening-thinking activity (the A → M), the readalong aspect of the A-V, and additional activities as included in "Teaching Reading Through Creative Movement." Later in the chapter a detailed specific lesson guideline will be given for one of the stories.

Preparing the Children for Listening

Set the Scene for Listening

The stories relate to the interest and the problems of children. Each story has a setting or experience that has a common element with the lives of children. Each story has a problem that

[5] Wilson, Humphrey, and Sullivan, *op. cit.*, pp. 5–8 of the Teacher's Guide.

touches upon a situation to which children can identify. The teacher should relate each story to the experiences of the children in order to call upon these experiences to make the story "come alive." Specific suggestions are made for each story that the teacher can develop to set the scene.

Develop Purposes for Listening

Children should be encouraged to formulate their own purposes for listening. As the teacher pursues the discussion of the story prior to listening (building interest but not giving story away) he or she should be alert to opportunities to help children identify their own purposes for listening. Suggested purposes for listening are presented for each story, as will be seen later in the example.

Children should be encouraged before listening to let the story and music "paint a picture" and to pretend they are part of the picture. (Appropriate musical backgrounds have been provided to enhance the mood of each story. Recent research has verified the contribution of music in learning to read.)[6]

Teacher Observation While Children Listen

Note Evidence of Involvement and Reaction to Story

Some insight into children's involvement and reaction to an experience may be gained by observing their physical and facial expressions. Spontaneous creative expression may be manifested in observable behavior. However, it can be deceptive when one watches children as they listen. It often appears that they are not paying attention due to excessive movement in their seats. The teacher should not be misled because sitting quietly is not a requisite for listening attentively. The teacher might wish to observe for the following behaviors.

1. Attentiveness, interest, anticipation.
2. Evidence of body movement response to story.
3. Reaction to story such as laughing, smiling, frowning.
4. Verbal comments.

[6] Movesian, Edwin: Reading music and reading words. *Today's Education, The Journal of the National Education Association,* Jan. 1969, pp. 42–43.

Reacting to the Story

Encourage Creative Movement

Following the listening to the story the children should be encouraged to talk about what they heard. Specific questions can be asked which might generate creative movement to act out what happened or to express how they feel. Many children will respond slowly when creative movement activities are suggested. The teacher should not be discouraged because they need time and encouragement. They may listen to the recording again and maybe even a third time. Children who want to create can do so while others observe. For some children the story may be too long. It is entirely appropriate to stop the record for some discussion and some creative movement. In fact, doing so sometimes generates interest for the remainder of the story.

Teachers have found several of the following techniques to be useful while working with children in creative movement.

1. All children can listen to the story and then be encouraged to react in a spontaneous manner. Little structure is needed. Children can move and react as they think about the story.
2. Children can react in small groups or pairs after they have listened to the story. Again, the reaction can be spontaneous.
3. The above suggestions can be used and the teacher can "trigger" the children with questions of the types indicated in each Lesson Guideline. (Refer to Sample Lesson Guideline later in the chapter)
4. Children may ask questions of other children who, in turn, respond with creative movement.
5. After any of the above techniques have been used, the teacher might play the section of the record which contains the music but not the story. Children may use it as a background as they act out what happened in the story or to express how they feel.

It has been found that too much teacher structure interferes with creative movement. Generally, it is felt that the teacher should be in the background. Children must develop the idea that they are not trying to please the teacher—just reacting as best they can to the story or the question. Likewise, rigid formations in which children stand in a circle tend to stifle creativity. Thus, informal and loose arrangement should be used.

Develop Understanding of Story

Whatever purposes were set for listening to the story, both teacher's and children's, should be discussed. Each story provides opportunity to develop certain types of comprehension skills—main idea, supporting details, organization, inference, critical evaluation, and vocabulary. Each specific Lesson Guideline includes ideas for discussion relative to these skills. The ideas presented are identified according to the type of comprehension skill receiving emphasis. Types of expressive movement that may be used to develop these skills are also identified. All of the ideas presented for discussion in the Lesson Guideline for each story should not necessarily be used with a given class. It is suggested that the teacher select one or more of the ideas according to their appropriateness for the skill needs of the group.

Teachers will probably wish to observe children for the following behaviors.

1. Can recall story elements from listening.
2. Indicates depth of comprehension from responses in discussion.
3. Shows freedom, creativeness in "acting out" elements of story.

From Listening to Reading

As the children listen to the stories and react to them they are developing essential skills for reading. Many of them will now find themselves ready to break the written code and read the stories. This is the A–V part, the last aspect of the AMAV technique. It is not important at this point to determine whether the children know all the words; rather, it *is* important that they understand that reading adds just one step (the breaking of the printed code) to what they have been doing and enjoying, that of listening to and interpreting stories. Several suggestions are offered to the teacher who feels that some of the children are ready for this step.

1. The children who desire to do so should be permitted to read along with the story as they listen to it. Normally such reading along will take place after they have heard the story in a Directed-Listening Activity. Some children may do this orally. Others will prefer to do it silently. Others may not prefer to do it at all. In any case, permitting them to have a book as they listen provides an opportunity for reading along.

2. Those who desire may be permitted to read the story independently. Again they may choose to do this orally or silently but without the aid of listening to the record. They will probably come to the teacher for help with a word now and then. The teacher can tell them the word and let them get on with their reading. This may be done on a buddy system.

3. After a child or a group of children have read along or read alone, the teacher may choose to develop several sight words with the children. A suggested technique is for the children to pick words from the story which they know and which they want to place in their word banks or on word cards. Words thus picked are written for the children (soon they will be able to copy the words themselves). After the children have selected several the teacher may pick a few to add to their collection. Note that children will tend to choose exciting words such as, *worried, laughed, lucky,* and *catch.* The point is, they have some words which they can read and which they are willing to study. The teacher will want to select several service words such as, *and, were,* and *here.*

4. Word reinforcement activities similar to those which are being used in reading instruction programs are now in order. Teams of two can read their words to each other. They can also match words. They can build sentences from their

words. As the number of words increase, opportunities become available for classifying words by action words, names of people, animals, and the like. Words can be filed in alphabetic order thus developing another needed skill.

5. When phonics lessons are taught the words which the children have learned come in handy. Instead of listing several words of the *b* sound, for example, the children can choose "*b*" words from their word cards. In such a manner the teacher is assuring that learning is going from the "know" to the "new."

6. Once the stories have been mastered, children will find it enjoyable to read them to others. They can take the story booklets home to read to little brothers and sisters, and they can read to each other.

There is some possibility that the stories can be overworked. However, if the teacher operates from the premise that children are choosing to involve themselves in these suggested activities, the chances of overworking these stories is held to a minimum.

Suggested Enrichment Activities

Utilize the Communicative Arts

After having listened to the stories, play a part of it and let the children develop alternate endings. These can be typed or printed and used as language experience stories.

Have children who desire, listen to the story at a listening station. Afterwards they may talk about what they think may happen next or might make up a play or skit to set out what they think might happen.

Utilize the Creative Arts

Children may want to dramatize portions or an entire story. Children may want to draw or paint pictures to illustrate any portion of the story. Children should be encouraged to use techniques such as cut or torn paper, collage, finger paint, or chalk as a variation from the crayon drawing. Children may want to make puppets or dioramas to put the story into three dimensions. Games and stunts relating to the different stories might be played during the activity periods.

Related Stories for Children

Extend Interest in Reading

Children should be encouraged to extend their reading beyond teacher-directed reading activities. Each Lesson Guideline lists several books on related themes for those children who would like to read another story much like the one they have enjoyed. Some books listed, while similar in theme, may be used to note differences or a new direction upon the theme.

Copies of these books should be on display in the classroom at the time the story is presented to the children. If the suggested books are not available the teacher should select other books related to the story themes. Children may then browse and select on their own a book or books that they want to read or for the teacher to read to them.

SAMPLE LESSON GUIDELINE[7]

Title of Story: HAROLD HOUND DOG

Harold Hound Dog lived on a farm.
He lived with his family.
It was a big family.
There were many Hound Dogs.
There was his father.
His name was Harry Hound Dog.
There was his mother.
Her name was Hilda Hound Dog.
There were many brothers.
There was Hector,
   and Harvey,
   and Homer
   and Hugo.
Oh yes, there was also Harold's grandfather.
His name was Old Herman Hound Dog.
Old Herman Hound Dog loved his grandchildren.

[7] Wilson, Humphrey, and Sullivan, *op. cit.*, pp. 35–41 of the Teacher's Guide.

But there was one thing he wished.
He wished that all of them would be good rabbit chasers.
He would say,
   "A Hound Dog must be a good rabbit chaser."
He told his grandchildren many stories.
He told stories of chasing rabbits.
He told how he chased rabbits.
He told how their father chased rabbits.
He told them how they must grow up to be good rabbit chasers
   too.
There was one Hound Dog who looked just like Grandfather.
That was Harold Hound Dog.
Grandfather thought Harold would be the best rabbit chaser
   of all.
One day he said, "Harold, you are just like your Grandfather.
You will be the best rabbit chaser of all."
"But Grandfather," replied Harold.
"But what, Harold?" asked Grandfather.
"Oh, nothing," answered Harold.
You see, Harold did not want to chase rabbits—
   not for real, that is.
He liked rabbits.
He thought they were nice.
He wanted to be their friend.
But who ever heard of that—
   a Hound Dog and a rabbit friends.
But how could he tell Grandfather?
He could not.
No, he just could not.
Harold was very sad.
He went off by himself and sat down under a tree.
He thought, and thought, and thought.
Suddenly he heard something.
He turned and looked around.
What do you think he saw?
Yes, it was a rabbit.
The rabbit was very close.
Harold did not want to frighten him.
Harold spoke softly.
"Hello," he said.
The rabbit jumped.
He looked around.
He was frightened.
Harold said, "Don't be afraid.

I won't hurt you.
I want to be your friend."
"But," said the rabbit, "You're a hound dog,
   and hound dogs chase rabbits,"
Harold replied, "Yes, I'm Harold Hound Dog.
But I don't want to chase rabbits—
   not for real, that is.
My Grandfather is Old Herman Hound Dog.
He wants me to be the best rabbit chaser of all.
But I don't want to.
I want to be your friend.
Will you be my friend?" asked Harold.
The rabbit was not sure, but he thought that maybe Harold
   really wanted to be his friend.
"All right," he answered.
We can be friends.
My name is Ricky Rabbit."
Ricky Rabbit told Harold about his friends.
There was Ralph Rabbit,
   and Rex,
   and Robert,
   and Roy,
   and Ronald.
And there were many other rabbits.
Harold Hound Dog asked,
   "Would they be my friends too?"
"I'm sure they would," replied Ricky Rabbit.
Ricky was sorry for Harold.
He knew that Harold did not want to be a rabbit chaser.
Ricky thought, "How could Harold chase rabbits—
   but not for real, that is?
Could he chase them and still be their friends?"
Suddenly Ricky had an idea.
"Why of course," thought Ricky.
He had thought of a way.
He remembered a game.
He had seen children play it.
They called the game "Hound and Rabbit."
One child would be the Hound.
The other children would be the Rabbits.
The hound would chase them.
When a child was caught he was the hound.
Ricky told Harold about the game.
He said, "You can play with my rabbit friends."
Harold thought it was fine.

He went into the woods with Ricky Rabbit.
He met Ricky's friends.
Harold Hound Dog told his story.
He told them he did not want to case them—
   not for real that is.
Ricky told them about the game.
They all said they would play.
So Harold Hound Dog played.
He played with all the rabbits.
He chased them—
   but not for real, that is.
They played and played.
Finally it was time to go home.
Harold said good-bye to his rabbit friends.
He started home.
He walked slowly.
He was very tired because he had played so long.
He had chased rabbits all day—
   but not for real, that is.

Preparing the Children for Listening

Set the Scene for Listening

HAROLD HOUND DOG deals with the problem of children sometimes being expected to fulfill the aspirations and dreams of the adults in their families which might not be their own. The following topics can be discussed:

1. Children's experiences with different kinds of dogs and different ways dogs hunt.
2. What parents want children to be when they grow up and what children hope to be.

Develop Purposes for Listening

If the children have not clearly established purposes for listening, the teacher can use the following purposes:

1. Listen to find out what is Harold Hound Dog's special problem. (Grandfather wants Harold to be something that Harold does not want to be.)
2. Listen to find out how Harold solves his problem. (Harold chases rabbits, but not for real, that is.)

3. Listen to be able to tell whether they think Harold has a good solution to his problem. (Any viewpoint by the children should be accepted. They should be encouraged nevertheless to be able to state why they feel as they do.)

Teacher Observation While Children Listen

Note Evidence of Involvement and Reaction to Story

Observe for evidence of such behavior as the following:

1. Attentiveness, interest, anticipation.
2. Evidence of body movement response to story.
3. Reaction to story such as laughing, smiling, frowning.
4. Verbal comments.

Reacting to the Story

Encourage Creative Movement

The children must first be encouraged to show how the story made them feel by reacting spontaneously. The children should also be encouraged to talk about the story. The teacher's specific questions might generate creative interpretation through movement. Children may act out what happened or express how they would feel if they were Harold Hound Dog, Grandfather, or Ricky Rabbit.

Develop Understanding of Story

Children's reaction to the purposes set for listening should be discussed. The following ideas are presented to develop various types of comprehension skills through creative movement when appropriate. The teacher should select *one or more* of these according to the needs of the particular group of children.

Comprehension Skill	Concept for Discussion	Type of Creative Movement
Main Idea	1. Children may name Harold Hound Dog's special problem. (not wanting to be a rabbit chaser like his grandfather)	Mimetic*

Specific Fact	2. Children can tell how Harold solved his problem. (Pretending to chase rabbits rather than doing it for real)	Mimetics

Vocabulary	3. Children can act out chasing rabbits to bring out meaning of meaning of the word *chase*. (Acting might include dog running, rabbit jumping.)	Mimetics
		Stunts:
		  Rabbit Jump
		  Puppy Dog Run

Organization	4. Children can identify the rules of the game, Hound and Rabbit. Rules may be written on the board. Children can play the game.	Game:
		  Hound and
		  Rabbit

Inference	5. Children should be able to identify story clues as to whether Old Herman Hound Dog was very old, as: a. He only dreamed of chasing rabbits. b. He is called Old Herman Hound Dog. (Children can show how Grandfather gathered grandchildren around him to tell stories.)	Mimetics
Inference	6. Children should be able to identify story clues as to whether Harold enjoyed playing with friends, as: a. He played until the end of the day. b. He was very tired and walked slowly. (Children can act out how Harold looked after playing hard)	Mimetics
	7. Question children as to whether there were *many* or *few* hound dogs in the story. They should bring out the difference between the meaning of the two words. Some children might identify the relativity of the meaning of these words in terms of larger groups. (Children can line up to represent Mother, Father, Grandfather, Hector, Harvey, Homer, Hugo, and Harold—eight in the family.) The children can decide whether this	

* The term "mimetic" literally means to "imitate." It is used here to mean that the child moves like or acts out something that he has heard about in the story. In some cases the child will be familiar with the particular movement, having seen it in his own experince. For example, most children have seen a puppy dog run; however, they may not have attempted to move in this manner.

	number would be *many* or *few*. Children can decide by grouping themselves how many hounds would represent *few*. Children could also decide whether there were *many* or *few* rabbits in the story.
Critical Evaluation	8. Children should determine whether Harold's solution to his problem was a good one and be able to support their conclusions.
Reaction	9. Children might also discuss whether they think their parents should expect children to become exactly what they want.

The teacher should observe for the following behaviors:

1. Can recall story elements from listening.
2. Indicate depth of comprehension from responses in discussion.
3. Show freedom, creativeness in "acting out" elements of story.

From Listening Experiences to Reading

Refer to the "Guideline" section (page 109) for ways children may wish to "read along" or "read alone" using the story booklets or for means of developing sight vocabulary and phonics skills.

Suggested Enrichment Activities

Refer to the "Guideline" section (page 111) for utilizing the communicative and the creative arts for children's means of reacting to the story.

Related Stories for Children

Refer to the "Guideline" section (page 112) for suggestions as to the use of supplementary and recreational reading as an extension of the teacher-directed listening activity. The following books are recommended for children in grades one through three. Some are suitable for children to read. Others are more appropriate for the teacher to read to the children.

Buckley, Helen E.: *Grandmother and I.* New York, Lothrop, 1961.

Hoban, Russell, and Garth Williams: *Bedtime for Frances.* New York, Harper & Row, Publishers, 1960.

Le Witt, Jan: *The Vegetabull.* New York, Harcourt, Brace & Co., 1956.

Peet, Bill: *Huge Harold.* Boston, Houghton, Mifflin Company, 1961.

Humphrey, James H., and Virginia Moore; *Read and Play Series.* Champaign, Ill., Garrard Publishing Co., 1962, and London, England, Frederick Muller Ltd., 1965. Set 1, Book 1 Roy Rabbit and His Friends, page 17. The Jumping Rabbit, page 33.

It should be readily discerned that the original work involved a vast amount of detail. Writing the original stories took a considerable amount of time as did the selection of appropriate musical background for the stories. Several tryouts of the material and numerous revisions of the Teacher's Guide were necessary to make the materials conform to the specifications and criteria established by the creators. However, it is possible for teachers to prepare their own materials to teach children to read through creative movement, using the AMAV Technique. Although such a procedure would not likely to be so detailed as the original work and is somewhat of a painstaking task, it can provide an interesting activity for a creative teacher. Preparing such materials can also be creative projects for older children. Remedial readers can help to prepare such stories for younger children.

CHAPTER EIGHT

DIAGNOSIS THROUGH MOTOR ACTIVITY

FOR CLASSROOM instruction to be both relevant and efficient increasing emphasis is being placed on the basing of learning activities on specific information regarding children's achievement as well as their interests, experience background, and style of learning. *Diagnostic teaching* is today's byword as school systems address their attention to meeting the individual needs of children. This applies particularly to reading instruction through the nationwide "Right to Read" program.

CLASSROOM DIAGNOSIS

Over the years the term *diagnosis* has generally been thought of as a more formal out-of-classroom procedure for those children the teacher identifies as having difficulties in their attempts to learn to read. Occasionally diagnosis is requested for those children whom teachers consider as not working up to their potential. But today, more and more specialists in reading are recognizing that in most cases classroom diagnosis can provide adequate information about the reading skill strengths and needs of children to help the classroom teacher make appropriate adjustments in instruction. Such adjustments involve focus on specific skills, levels of material, and method of instruction.

Classroom diagnosis has been directed to assessing the skill strengths and needs of children, either prior to or after instruction. Traditional measures have been standardized tests (usually survey in nature), informal inventories, or teacher-made tests. In recent years the value of teacher observations of children during different types of reading situations has been recognized as essential to supplement information received from the traditional measures. Such observations are followed by recording and analyzing their reading performance. According to Austin, "Today, few educators fail to recognize that continuous, functional assessment is an essential ingredient for the total school program."[1]

The procedure of observing, recording, and analyzing a child's performance during the learning activity has come to be recognized as perhaps a more reliable assessment of his skills development. Such procedures have become the framework for diagnostic teaching. Bond has described diagnostic teaching as being "based on an understanding of the *reading* strengths and needs of each child. These knowledges must be used to modify instructional procedures so that teaching, adjusted to the changing needs of the children, can be maintained. Such teaching is based on continuous diagnosis of the skill development of each child."[2] It is at this point that the use of motor activities can play a unique role in diagnosis.

One of the many problems inherent in testing situations is the effect of a child's apprehension on his performance of the task involved. Basic principles of clinical diagnosis in reading have alluded to this problem by emphasizing the importance of establishing rapport with the child, starting the testing with less threatening types of tasks, and stopping at the frustration level before complete discouragement disintegrates the testing situation. Teachers using such classroom diagnosis measures as mentioned often voice a concern relating to this apprehension on the part of the children. They realize that the child must be put at ease as to the nature and the reason for testing. Paper and pencil tests throughout the grades, along with the aptitude tests and college entrance examinations, have resulted

[1] Austin, Mary C.: Strategies for evaluating reading programs: elementary level. Liebert, Robert (Ed.): *Diagnostic Viewpoints in Reading*. Newark, Delaware, International Reading Association, 1971.

[2] Bond, Guy L.: Diagnostic teaching in the classroom. DeBoer, Dorothy L. (Ed.): *Reading Diagnosis and Evaluation*. Newark, Delaware, International Reading Association, 1970. pp. 130–131.

in adult aversion to test-taking to the point of significant blocking of what might well be a usual performance level of an individual when not under stress.

Diagnostic Teaching Techniques

Diagnostic teaching techniques employing observation, recording, and analysis of children's performance in day-to-day reading situations has become a significant trend in assessment. Obtaining daily feedback is a key to structuring appropriate day-to-day learning activities, because they are based on the "real" reading performance of the child. It is a better "reading" of where the child is in his skills development. Therefore, in diagnostic teaching, teachers are using such techniques as coding errors made by children while oral reading to prove points in the discussion of material they are reading for a Directed Reading-Thinking Activity. In this way the teacher has information about the children's sight vocabulary, word attack application to unfamiliar words in context reading, and comprehension skills.

The every-pupil-response technique is used by the teacher as a diagnostic teaching procedure in many types of situations. With the technique calling for each child in a group to respond to a question or problem by holding up an answer card or signaling with a finger response a choice of answers, the teacher is able to check the performance of all the children. The teacher can observe each child's understanding and interpreting of the material, his application of a specific skill to new words as in the case of reading. This technique not only provides information about each child's skills development within a group activity, but it also involves each child consistently throughout the learning and application of skills. This aspect of maximum involvement of each child within a group activity is particularly inherent in motor activities. An example of this is the game Match Cats which is described later in the chapter.

Teachers are also using games as a means of assessing the level of mastery of skills to determine whether further instructional activities need to be planned. Such reading games have been essentially *passive* in nature rather than *active*. The techniques as described for diagnostic teaching have served the teacher well in efforts to develop a reading program that meets the individual needs of the children.

It is interesting to note that these diagnostic techniques are geared to observing an individual child's performance within group learning activities. Teachers employing these techniques have reported they are better able to plan further activities for children to meet their individual needs through subgrouping children for additional learning experiences. As a result, the individualizing of instruction, a major objective of schools, becomes a reality.

Motor Activities as a Diagnostic Teaching Technique

As previously mentioned, the unique role of motor activities in classroom diagnosis becomes evident when games, as a diagnostic teaching technique are discussed. By adding the dimension of motor involvement to game activities the use of children's naturally physically-oriented world becomes a positive factor operating to facilitate further interest as well as more involvement and attending to the learning task. Many children tend to lose their apprehension of an intellectual task when it is "buried" in the context of a motor activity.

In particular, disabled readers will often perform tasks such as auditory and visual discrimination while playing a game like Man from Mars, Match Cards, and Letter Spot* when they would be saying "I can't do it" in more traditional learning activities. *Active* games tend to draw out the reluctant learner even more than *passive* games. Observation of children with severe reading problems, whose discouragement and frustration initially hampers their willingness even to participate, has found their natural affinity for physical activity has been the starting point of a more accurate assessment of their skill strengths and needs as well as remediation.

The total physical involvement of such children in motor ac-

---

* Descriptions of these games, and others, are presented later in this chapter.

tivities related to reading, as discussed in the previous chapters, appears to act as a means for releasing the emotional blockage that inhibits any attempt to perform the intellectual reading tasks involved. And once these children participate successfully in such activities because of the strengthening of input through their physical world, the process of building more positive attitudes toward reading and a feeling that they can learn is begun. Needless to say, once the teacher has observed a higher-level performance of children in this setting it is important to help the children recognize that they were able, and did, perform the skill involved. Such children need to be shown they *can* and *have* mastered a skill with specific evidence that they have learned.

While the initial focus of motor activities has been on *active* games as useful diagnostic tools, motor-oriented reading materials and creative movement activities are also conducive to diagnosis. Once again the teacher is able to observe children demonstrate a level of skills development from the reading tasks utilized in the activity in a natural setting.

Four important factors in motor activities that the teacher utilizes to determine whether further learning experiences are necessary for skill mastery are (1) the type of sensory input or modality involved in the reading task inherent in the motor activity, (2) the accuracy of the child's responses in the reading task, (3) the reaction time of children in performing that reading task, and (4) the self-evaluation of the child of his performance.

Sound instructional programs have always been specific-skill oriented. The impact of establishing behaviorally-stated goals as objectives for instruction has helped teachers to move beyond such lesson plan goals as "learning word attack skills" to "being able to identify by name the initial letter of a word given orally" or "being able to give orally another word that begins with the same sound as a word presented visually." In the latter lesson objectives both input and output modality are clearly stated so that a teacher observing such activities can analyze children's performance in regard to sensory modality both for input and output production. Such information helps the teacher to identify those children who consistently give evidence of significant differences in performance when lesson input is basically auditory or visual. Such information helps the teacher to adapt instruction accordingly and thereby assure more meaningful, and more successful, learning-to-read experiences. Examples of different modalities used are two games. In the game, "Crows and Cranes," the input is auditory while in the game, "Black and White," the input is visual. Both of these were described in Chapter Four.

Motor activities related to reading by their nature enable the teacher to identify the specific reading skill involved. The reading skills utilized in motor activities as described in previous chapters can be readily identified. An example of this would be the game Letter Spot in which the reading skill is one of visual recognition of upper and lower case letters in order to play the game.

The second factor in motor activities which a teacher utilizes is the accuracy of children's responses to the reading tasks inherent in the activity. It can be observed those children who use the specific skill with at least 90 per cent accuracy in their responses. This should represent skill mastery at the independent level. Any lower percentage of accuracy would indicate additional experiences are necessary.

The third factor relating to the reaction time of children's performance during motor activities helps the teacher to identify the ease and comfort of children in performing a specific task. Reaction time in the present text refers to the amount of time it takes for the onset of a response of a person after receiving a stimulus. By observing the quickness of a child's response to the reading task inherent in the motor activity the teacher can assess the degree of ease as well as the accuracy of the child's responses. While percentage of accuracy is a useful and necessary tool in determining when a child reaches the point of skill mastery, the ease and comfort of the child during the reading task is also a significant factor. Skill mastery implies operation at an "automatic" level independently.

Of particular concern in consideration of reaction time are

those children who have a disability in processing the sensory input with a resulting delay in reaction to the question or task presented. Such impairment can effect auditory, visual or feeling input. This may be related to the first factor in use of motor activities as a diagnostic tool in which the teacher is observing children's performance in terms of modality used. In the game, "Call and Catch," the teacher adjusts the timing by momentarily holding the ball before throwing it in the air. This game is described later in the chapter. In the case of reaction time there may simply be a lesser degree of impairment resulting only in more reaction time necessary to perform the task. The teacher must be aware that children may have this type of disability and attempt to recognize those children who consistently need additional time to respond to the task. It is important to adjust to the needs of such children rather than categorizing their delay in responding as being the result of disinterest or uncooperativeness. Motor activities can easily be adapted to such children.

The fourth factor is that of self-evaluation by the children themselves. Children should be encouraged not only to react to the activity itself but also to assess how they did and what they might do to improve their performance of the reading skill involved. It might be a case of looking more carefully at the word, picture, or design cards used in the game. In such pleasurable activities children appear more willing to examine their performance in the learning tasks involved, and quite realistically as well.

The uniqueness of motor activities, therefore, as another means of classroom diagnosis, is that such activities tend to remove the apprehension of testing procedures and can demonstrate a level of skills development that is possibly more consistent with day-to-day performance. Such performance of the reading skill involved in the motor activity might even appear higher than when the children are engaged in more traditional reading activities. This higher level performance should then be taken as a more accurate assessment of children's potential level of performance when they are operating under optimum conditions of learning.

DIAGNOSIS OF READING READINESS SKILLS

Reading readiness skills are a complex cluster of basic skills including (1) language development in which the child learns to transform *his experience* with *his environment* into language symbols through listening, oral language facility and a meaningful vocabulary; (2) the skills relating to the mechanics of reading such as left-to-right orientation, auditory and visual discrimination, and recognition of letter names and sounds; and (3) the cognitive processes of comparing, classifying, ordering, interpreting, summarizing, and imagining.

Likewise, sensorimotor skills provide a foundation for these basic skills by sharpening the senses and developing motor skills involving spatial, form, and time concepts. The following outline identifies some concepts developed through direct body movement:

(1) Body Image* (body parts, relating body and body parts to the environment, movement with body parts, usage of body parts)
(2) Space and Direction (children point, move to objects)
(3) Balance
(4) Basic Body Movements (see Chapter Six)
(5) Eye-Hand Coordination (ball bouncing, batting balloons, bean bag or ring toss, hammering nails)
(6) Eye-Foot Coordination (propelling ball with feet and following foot tracks)
(7) Form Perception
(8) Rhythm
(9) Large Muscle Activity
(10) Fine Muscle Activity (finger strength, coordination and fine eye muscular movement).

These skills are essential to the establishment of a sound foundation for the beginning-to-read experiences of children. Not only can the reading readiness program, structured for the development of these skills, be facilitated through motor activities, but diagnosis of progress in skills development can be obtained

---

* The game Busy Bee which was described in Chapter Four shows how body image can be improved.

by teacher observation and children's self-evaluation from the motor activities. Such physically-oriented activities as chasing and fleeing games, games of circle formation, stationary relays, rhythmic activities, singing games, story plays and mimetic activities can be utilized effectively to provide meaningful and satisfying learning activities in the reading readiness program. Chapters Five, Six, and Seven present ways to implement these types of motor activities. The following games are described to indicate the variety of activities that may be employed in the development and assessment of readiness skills.

Language Development

In such games as I'm Tall, I'm Small* and the following games, concept formation is translated into a meaningful vocabulary.

Concept: Classification

Activity: Pet Store

One fairly large Pet Store is marked off at one end of the activity area and a Home at the other end. At the side is a Cage. In the center of the playing area stands the Pet Store Owner. All the children stand in the Pet Store and are given a picture of one kind of pet (for example, fish, bird, dog). There should be about two or three pictures of each kind of pet. The Pet Store Owner calls "Fish" (or any of the other pets in the game). The children who have pictures of fish must try to run from the Pet Store to their new Home without being caught or tagged by the Owner. If they are caught, they must go to the Cage and wait for the next call. The game continues until all the Pets have tried to get to their new home. Kinds of pets can be changed frequently.

Application:

By grouping themselves according to the animal pictures, children are able to practice classifying things that swim, things

* This game is described in Chapter Five.

that fly, and so forth. At the end of the game the class can count how many fish, dogs, and so forth were caught. All the fish, birds, dogs, and so forth can then form their own line to *swim, fly,* or *walk* back to the Pet Store, where new pictures can be given to the children for another game.

Concept: Vocabulary Meaning—Action Words

Activity: What to Play

The children may stand beside their desks. One of the children is selected to be the leader. While that child is coming to the front of the room to lead, the rest of the class begins to sing:

> Mary tell us what to play,
> What to play, what to play,
> Mary tell us what to play,
> Tell us what to play.

(The song is sung to the tune of Mary Had a Little Lamb.) The leader then says, "Let's play we're fishes," or "Let's wash dishes," or "Let's hold a doll." She then performs some action that the other children have to imitate. On a signal the children stop, and a new leader is selected.

Application:

This game gives children an opportunity to act out meanings of words. It helps them to recognize that spoken words represent actions of people as well as things that can be touched.

Concept: Vocabulary Meaning—Left and Right

Activity: Changing Seats

Enough chairs for each child in the group are placed side by side in about four or five rows. The children sit alert, ready to move either way. The teacher calls, "Change right!" and each child moves into a seat to his right. When the teacher calls "Change left!" each child moves left. The child at the end of the row who does not have a seat to move to must run to the other end of his row to sit in the vacant seat there. The teacher can bring excitement to the game by the quickness of commands or unexpectedness by calling the same direction several times in succession. After each command the first row of children who all find seats may score a point for that row.

Application:

This type of activity makes children more aware of the necessity of differentiating left from right. At the beginning of the game, children may not be able to differentiate directions rapidly. The teacher will need to gear the rapidity of her commands according to the skills of the group.

Auditory Discrimination

The following activity shows not only an active game using auditory discrimination skills but also the way games can be adapted to other reading skills.

Concept: Auditory Discrimination—Beginning Sounds of Words

Activity: Man from Mars

One child is selected to be the Man from Mars and stands in the center of the activity area. The other children stand behind a designated line at one end of the play area. The game begins when the children call out, "Man from Mars, can we chase him through the stars? The teacher answers, "Yes, if your name begins like duck." (Or any other word.) All the children whose name begins with the same beginning sound as *duck* or whatever word is called, chase the Man from Mars until he is caught. The child who tags him becomes the new Man from Mars, and the game continues.

Application:

In order for the children to run at the right time, they must listen carefully and match beginning sounds. If the teacher sees a child not running when he should, individual help can be given. Children can also listen for words beginning like or ending like other words the teacher may use for the key word.

Visual Discrimination

The various games described here relating to visual discrimination indicate the variety of active game situations which can be utilized to develop skills or to assess skills development.

Concept: Visual Discrimination

Activity: Match Cats

The teacher makes duplicate sets of cards with pictures or designs on them with as many cards as there are children. The children sit on the floor. The cards are passed out randomly. On a signal or music playing, the children move around the play area with a specified locomotor movement such as hopping or skipping. When the music stops or a signal is given, each child finds the person with his duplicate card, joins one hand, and they sit on the floor together. The last couple down becomes the Match Cats for that turn. The children then get up and exchange cards. The game continues in the same manner with different locomotor movements used.

Application:

Depending on the level of skills development of the children, the cards may be pictures of real objects or abstract forms, colors, alphabet letters, and words.

Concept: Visual Discrimination

Activity: Mother May I (An adaptation)

The children stand on a line at the back of the activity area. The teacher has cards showing object pairs, similar and different. The teacher holds up one pair of cards. If the paired objects or symbols are the same, the children may take one giant step forward. Any child who moves when he sees an unpaired set of cards must return to the starting line. The object of the game is to reach the finish line on the opposite side of the playing area.

Application:

The teacher may select cards to test any level of visual discrimination. Using pairs of cards for categorizing pictures would utilize concept and language development.

Concept: Visual Discrimination

Activity: Match Cards

Each child in the group is given a different-colored card. Several children are given duplicate cards. There are two chairs placed in the center of the activity area. On a signal the children may walk, skip, hop, etc., to the music around the play area. When the music stops the teacher holds up a card. Those children whose cards match the teachers card run to sit in the chairs. Anyone who got a seat scores a point. The play resumes. Cards should be exchanged frequently among the children.

Application:

This visual discrimination activity can be adapted easily to include increasing complexity of the visual discrimination task as well as how the children move about and the task for scoring points. Visual discrimination tasks might also include shapes, designs, letters (both capital and lower case).

Letter Recognition

Various levels of letter recognition skills are provided for by adaptations of the following games.

Concept: Recognizing Letters of the Alphabet

Activity: Letter Spot

Pieces of paper with lower case letters are placed in various spots around the floor or play area. There should be several pieces of paper with the same letters. The teacher has a number of large posters with the same but capital letters. (The overhead projector may be used to present letters in many letter styles, sizes, and colors). A poster is shown to the class. The children must identify the letter by name and then run to that letter on the floor. Any child who is left without a spot gets a point against him. Any child who has less than five points at the end of the period is considered a winner.

Application:

Children are helped to associate letters with their names. After the game the posters can be put on display around the room.

Concept: Recognizing Letters of the Alphabet

Activity: Call and Catch (variation)

The children stand in a circle. The teacher stands in the center of the circle with a rubber ball. Each child is assigned a different letter. The letter may be written on a card attached to a string which the child wears as a necklace. Each child reads his letter before the game is started. The teacher calls out a letter and throws the ball into the air. The child who has that letter tries to catch the ball after it bounces. The teacher can provide for individual differences of children. For the slower child the teacher can call the letter and then momentarily hold the ball before throwing it in the air.

Application:

This activity provides children the opportunity to become familiar with names and visual identification of letters. Later the teacher could hold up letter cards rather than calling the letter. The children might then have to name the letter and catch the ball. Eventually both upper and lower case cards might be used in the activity.

DIAGNOSIS OF READING SKILLS

As the child moves into the beginning reading skills, motor activities continue to serve as a means both for developing and reinforcing skills as well as providing a valuable means of assessing skill mastery. Skill areas as sight vocabulary, word attack skills, alphabetical order, comprehension, and vocabulary meaning can be developed through the many dimensions of motor activities previously described in Chapters Five, Six, and Seven. Likewise, level of skill mastery can also be assessed. Games that utilize the various reading skills mentioned above are described in order to demonstrate the nature of active games that can be employed.

Sight Vocabulary

Developing sight vocabulary through active games utilizes words and phrases from materials children are currently reading.

Concept: Sight Vocabulary

Activity: Call Phrase

The children form a circle, facing the center. They may be seated or standing. One child is designated as the caller and stands in the center of the circle. Each child is given a card with a phrase printed on it. Several children can have the same phrase. The caller draws a card from a box containing corresponding phrase cards and holds up the card for everyone to see. When he reads the phrase, this is the signal for those children in the circle with the same phrase to exchange places before the caller can fill in one of the vacant places in the circle. The remaining child becomes the caller.

Application:

Children need opportunities to develop quick recognition of phrases. This game provides the repetition necessary to help children develop familiarity with phrases they are meeting in their reading material. The phrases may be taken from group experience stories, readers, or children's own experience stories.

Concept: Sight Vocabulary

Activity: Word Erase

The children are divided into several teams. The teams make rows at a specified distance from a blackboard. Previously the teacher has written lists of words from children's experience stories and readers, one for each team. On a signal the first child on each team calls the first word. If he is correct, as determined by the teacher, he runs to the board and erases it, then returns to the rear of his team. If he does not know the word, he may ask for help from one member of his team. The second child continues in the same manner. The game is won by the first team finished.

Application:

Words selected for this game may come from experience stories and stories read on that or the previous day. These games provide the necessary repetition to develop instant recognition of words and can be used to maintain words in addition to word banks and word games that the children utilize in the classroom.

Word Attack

Word attack skills that may be developed and assessed through active games may include phonic elements of words, rhyming words, vowel letter patterns, syllables, and endings. The Ending Relay previously described in Chapter Five provides reinforcement of structural analysis skills.

Concept: Auditory Discrimination-Consonant Digraphs (ch,sh,th)

Activity: Mouse and Cheese

A round mousetrap is formed by the children standing in a circle. In the center of the mousetrap is placed the cheese, a ball, or some other object. The children are then assigned one of the consonant digraphs *sh*, *ch*, or *th*. When the teacher calls a word beginning with a consonant digraph, all the children with this digraph run around the circle and back to their original place, representing the holes in the trap. Through these original places they run into the circle to get the cheese. The child who gets the cheese is the winning mouse for that turn. Another word is called, and the same procedure is followed. Children may be reassigned digraphs from time to time.

Application:

Children need repetition for developing the ability to hear and identify various sound elements within words. This game enables children to recognize consonant digraphs within the context of whole words. A variation of this game would be to have the teacher hold up word cards with words beginning with consonant digraphs rather than saying the word. This variation would provide emphasis on visual discrimination of initial consonant digraphs. Another variation would focus on ending consonant digraphs, either auditory or visual recognition.

Concept: Rhyming Words

Activity: Rhyme Chase

The children form a circle. Each child is given a card with a familiar word from the children's sight vocabulary written on it. The teacher may ask each child to pronounce his word before beginning the game. The children should listen and look at the words as each one identifies his word. The teacher then calls out a word that rhymes with one or several of the words held by the children. The child (or children) holds up his rhyming word so all the children can see it. He must then give another word that rhymes with his word. This is a signal for all the other children to run to a safety place previously designated by the teacher. The child (or children) with the rhyming words try to tag any one of the other children before he reaches a safe place. A child who is tagged receives a point. The object is for the children to get the lowest score possible. Word cards may be exchanged among the children after several turns.

Application:

In this activity the children are called upon to relate auditory experiences in rhyming with visual presentations of these words. Sight vocabulary is also emphasized as the children reinforce the concept of visual patterns in rhyming words.

Concept: Recognition of Visual Letter Patterns - Vowel Sound Principles (Open, Closed, Final *e*)

Activity: Letter Pattern Change

The children remain in their seats. Each child is given a card with a single-syllable word having one of the three vowel sound patterns (Examples: open-syllable pattern—a, he, go; closed-syllable pattern—get, bud, hip; final *e* pattern—game, lute, side). The teacher then holds up a word card with words also representing these patterns. Those children having words with the same letter pattern and the same vowel run to the board and write their word on the board and say it. Each child who is correct scores a point. Children may keep their own scores. Word cards should be changed frequently among the children. Later, the teacher may have the children whose word has the same letter pattern come to the board without it having to have the same vowel.

Application:

This game provides children the opportunity to practice recognition of visual letter patterns as cues to vowel sounds. Children can be called upon to identify the name of the vowel sound principle that their word represents, for example open, closed, or final *e*. The vowel digraph letter pattern might also be included in this activity.

Alphabetical Order

Alphabetizing words is an essential skill for locating words in dictionaries or information in encyclopedias. Active games utilizing the first two, three, or four letters for alphabetizing can later be developed as the teacher assesses when there is skill mastery of the less difficult tasks of alphabetizing.

Concept: Alphabetical Order

Activity: Alphabet Line-Up.

The class is divided into two teams. For each team a set of twenty-six cards, one for each letter of the alphabet, is placed out of order on the chalk tray at the front of the room or pinned to a bulletin board. The teams make rows at a specified distance from the letter display. A goal line is established at the back of the room for each team. The object of the game is for each member, one at a time, to run to pick a letter in correct alphabetical order, carry it to the teams goal line, and place the letter side by side in correct order. When each team member has found a letter, the team begins again until the alphabet is complete. The first team to complete placing the alphabet correctly at its goal line wins.

Application:

Children need many different types of opportunity to practice putting the letters in correct alphabetical order. This game provides a new activity to practice this skill.

Comprehension

Vocabulary meaning* as well as other comprehension skills such as in the following game utilizing sequence of events can be emphasized in motor activities. Sentence Relay further serves as an example of how the buddy system can work in the active game approach.

Concept: Sequence of Events

Activity: Sentence Relay

Relay teams of five children each are selected to make rows before a starting line ten to fifteen feet from sentence charts for each team. The remaining children can serve as scorers. Each child on the team is given a sentence that fits into an overall sequence for the five sentences given a team. (The teams are given duplicate sentences.) Each sentence gives a clue to its position in the sentence sequence, either by idea content or word clue. On a given signal the team members get together and decide the correct sentence order. The child with the first sentence then runs to the sentence chart, places his sentence on the top line of the chart, underlines the key part of the sentence that

---

* "I'm Tall, I'm Small," "What to Play," and "Changing Seats" are games presented earlier in chapter which reinforce vocabulary meaning.

gives the clue to the sequence, and returns to his team. The child with the next sentence then runs to place his sentence below the first sentence. This procedure continues until the sentences are in order. The team to complete the story with sentences in correct order first wins. The scorers check on the accuracy of the sentence order for each team. For the next game the scorers can exchange places with those who were on teams. Variations of this game can include the use of cartoons with each child being given one frame of the cartoon strip. To make the game more difficult, more sentences may be added to the sequence. To prevent copying, the teacher can give different story sentences to each team.

Application:

In this game those children having difficulty with reading are helped by those who are more able readers and not eliminated from the game. After each game the teacher should go over key elements in the sentences that provided clues to the proper sequence.

How might Sentence Relay be used for diagnostic purposes? It might be used just as it is described above or certain adaptations might be made. In this case, the reading task in the active game is to recognize key elements in the sentences that provide clues to the proper sequence. The teacher can note whether a child is able to identify appropriate clues to sequence in his sentence. The teacher might observe which children perform the task easily and those who appear to need additional experiences in identifying key elements in sentences relating to sequence.

The game might also be adapted by changing the game to one that utilizes a story with several key sentences missing, the number of missing sentences being the same as the number of chilren on each team. The reading task would then be one of using context clues of a larger meaning unit to identify the proper order of sentences.

One of the many advantages of the active games approach is that it is fairly easy for the teacher to identify the specific reading skills being utilized in a game which in turn facilitates assessment of children's mastery of that skill. In this way diagnostic teaching techniques aid a teacher's efforts to adjust the learning activities of the reading program to the needs of the children. The examples presented are representative of almost unlimited possibilities in structuring appropriate reading experiences for children. The creative teacher should be able to develop numerous activities by adapting those presented in the present text to the developmental level and skill needs of the children.

AUTHOR INDEX

143

SUBJECT INDEX